ELBERT HUBBARD

ELBERT HUBBARD

A TREASURY

OF REFLECTIONS ON LOVE, LABOR, LAUGHTER & LIFE

edited and introduced by

SAM TORODE

www.ElbertHubbard.org

TABLE OF CONTENTS

INTRODUCTION   *i*

I. LOVE

Making a Home   1
Happiness Lies in Equality   1
A Marriage of Minds   2
The Woman Who Understands   3
Women's Freedom   4
Patriarchal Marriage:
  the Death of Passion   5
Freedom & Obedience in Marriage   5
Love, Human & Divine   6
The Power of Love   7
Love & Death   7
Love for Love's Sake   8

II. LEARNING

Practical Education: A Manifesto   9
Teaching in Season   10
Education that Works   10
Education through Expression   11

Education through Travel   11
College & Character   12
The School of Life   13

III. LABOR

Worker's Creed   15
The Dignity of Labor   15
The Poverty of the Rich   16
The Basis of Business   16
Business as Public Service   17
Do Good Work   17
Salvation Through Action   17
Work, Health, Study   18
Work Is for the Worker   19
"Busyness"   19
Systems for Success   20
Innovation vs. Inertia   20
From Resources to Wealth   20
Art & Commerce   21
Women in the Economy   21
Thrift   21
Success by Nature   22

iv. Creed

My Creed 23

We Are One 24

What Is the Soul? 25

The Religion of Humanity 25

A Religion of Kindness 27

Evolving Beliefs 27

Evolving People 28

Live Now and Here 29

Redeeming Past Mistakes 29

Salvation 30

Damnation 30

The World Is Getting Better 31

From Darkness to Light 32

Holy Books 32

The Folly of Theology 33

The Unknowable 34

The Known 34

Childish Explanations 35

The Benefits of Sin 35

The Song of Songs 36

Rational Judaism 37

A Prayer of Gratitude 38

Ten Positive Commandments 39

A Prayer to Radiate Life 39

v. Country

Shrines of Liberty 41

Franklin 42

Sacajawea 42

John Brown 43

Thoreau 43

Yellowstone 44

The Business of War &
    the Art of Peace 44

Leave Us Alone! 46

Why I Am an Anarchist 48

Unjust Laws 49

Electing a Messiah 50

New Worlds to Conquer 50

vi. Character

Habits Create Character 53

Make Motion Equal Emotion 53

Make Action Equal Energy 54

Make Expression Equal
    Impression 55

Industry, Concentration
    & Self-Reliance 56

Initiative 57

Genius 57

Sympathy 58

The Ability to Say No 58

You Are What You Think 58

The Universe Within 59

The Cultured Mind 59

Meditation 60

Time 60

vii. Exercise

The Health Habit 61

The Wisdom of Symptoms 61

Happiness & Health 62

Age & Activity 63

The Fountain of Youth 63

Nature's Medicine 64

Horseback Riding 64

Health & Fear 65

Doctrine & Disease 66

VIII. EXPRESSION

Art & Understanding   67
Sex & Beauty   67
Artistic Conscience   68
The Power of Words   69
Literature & Light   69
The Great Writer   69
Poetry   70
A Voice that Inspires   70
Art & Advertising   70
Art & Economy   71

IX. INDIVIDUALITY

Some Mocked, Some Believed   73
Make Room for Individuality   74
Suppressing Genius   74

Individual Freedom   75
The Tyranny of Fashion   75
Live Your Own Life   75
The Courage to Change   76

X. INTERDEPENDENCE

A Declaration of Interdependence   77
Strength in Others   78
Friendship   78
Consider the Bee   79
The Spirit of the Hive   80
The Genius of Groups   80
The Community of Truth-Seekers   81

THE ROYCROFT IDEA   83
A STORY OF THE TITANIC   97

INTRODUCTION

A FORGOTTEN SAGE

TEN years ago, in a Texas antique shop, I happened upon a beautifully-bound, gilt-edged book titled *Elbert Hubbard of East Aurora*. It was the biography of a person apparently well-known in the early twentieth century, but of whom I'd never heard. This man Hubbard had written and published his own books—and since that was my own line of work, I bought the biography.

Such was my introduction to Elbert Hubbard (1856–1915), a fascinating and unjustly forgotten American sage.

The son of a country doctor, Hubbard grew up on an Illinois farm. He worked his way up from traveling soap salesman to become a partner in the Larkin Soap Company of Buffalo, New York, where he created innovative marketing campaigns.

But Hubbard's goals were greater than selling soap. Cashing in his Larkin shares, he traveled to Europe, where he sought out and met many of his heroes, including William Morris, founder of the Arts & Crafts movement. Inspired by Morris, upon returning Hubbard founded his own Arts & Crafts shop in the village of East Aurora, New York.

Established in 1895, Hubbard called his shop the Roycroft—meaning "king-craft," or crafts fit for a king. He hired skilled workers to make leather goods, metalware, furniture, stained glass, and more. A print shop was added to make hand-bound books, beginning with Hubbard's account of his travels in Europe and America, *Little Journeys to the Homes of Good Men & Great*.

Soon the Roycroft press began publishing Hubbard's own magazine, called *The Philistine* (so titled to indicate his opposition to the prevailing literary establishment). This provided a national reach both for Hubbard's writings and advertisements of Roycroft goods.

At its height, the Roycroft employed over five hundred people and attracted many notable visitors, including Tuskegee Institute founder Booker T. Washington, future Scopes trial lawyer Clarence Darrow, *Red Badge of Courage* author Stephen Crane, and automobile titan Henry Ford.

Hubbard's fame grew with the publication of his essay "A Message to Garcia" in 1898. It recounts the story of Andrew Rowan, a U.S. Army lieutenant who crossed hostile territory in Cuba to deliver a message to a rebel commander named Garcia. From this, Hubbard drew the moral of an employee who carries out his leader's orders immediately and without question, doing whatever it takes to get the job done. The heads of U.S. corporations saw the potential of this essay to inspire loyalty and industry in their employees, and so they ordered reprints by the hundreds-of-thousands.

A Message to Garcia became an instant and enduring bestseller. On its own, however, it fails to represent Hubbard's full philosophy. While certainly a proponent of hard work, Hubbard had equally strong convictions about individual freedom, originality, questioning authority, and determining one's own life rather than

> **The best service a book can render is not to impart truth, but to make you think it out for yourself.**

blindly following orders.

Over the years, Hubbard wrote short pieces on all subjects of importance to him—his ideas about business, labor, education, his personal philosophy (nearest to Ralph Waldo Emerson's Transcendentalism), and more. Most controversially, he argued in favor of pacifism and women's rights, and against traditional religious beliefs. This ran afoul of the guardians of culture and morality, and Hubbard was charged with distributing "obscene and objectionable" materials. He pleaded guilty and paid the $100 fine, but later was granted a presidential pardon.

In 1901, Hubbard's life was rocked by scandal. His marriage of twenty years ended after it was revealed that he'd fathered a child out-of-wedlock with Alice Moore, a feminist and suffragette whom he considered to be his true soul mate. Elbert and Alice married in 1904; they stayed in love and worked together closely until their deaths.

In 1915, the Hubbards embarked to Europe on the ship Lusitania. With a world war looming on the horizon, Hubbard sought to meet with Kaiser William II of Germany in hopes of finding common ground and preventing senseless bloodshed. The meeting never happened, alas, as the Lusitania was torpedoed by a German submarine and sank off the coast of Ireland.

Elbert and Alice Hubbard were last seen arm-in-arm, entering a room on the top deck of the ship, so they would die together rather than be parted in the waters.

As the inscription on their monument at the Roycroft campus says, "They lived and died fearlessly."

Since first picking up Hubbard's biography (written by his personal assistant, Felix Shay, and published in 1926), I've gone on to collect other Roycroft books. They are all beautifully crafted, and Hubbard's essays are inspiring and provocative.

All of Hubbard's works are out of print today except for "A Message to Garcia," and, in the original volumes, sometimes his true gems of thought are hidden among ephemeral musings.

With this treasury, I wish to bring those gems out of the shadows. I selected my favorite essays from Hubbard's works, titled them (most were originally published without titles), and arranged them by theme. In a few cases, I combined the best passages from separate but similar essays.

Hubbard was a master of the aphorism—the pithy, memorable saying—and these are set in the quote boxes throughout this book, beginning with the one on the facing page.

Finally, where it was possible to do so unobtrusively, I changed Hubbard's use of the words "man" and "men" to "humanity" and "people" when referring to all human beings. As a champion of equal rights, surely Hubbard would have used inclusive language were he writing today.

—Sam Torode
Nashville, Tennessee, 2016

Elbert and Alice Hubbard
with daughter Miriam

I.

LOVE

MAKING A HOME

IT requires two to make a home. The first home was made when a woman, cradling her loving arms around a baby, crooned a lullaby. All the tender sentimentality we throw around a place is the result of the sacred thought that we live there with someone else. It is our home. The home is a tryst—the place where we retire and shut the world out.

Lovers make a home, just as birds make a nest, and unless a man knows the spell of the divine passion I can hardly see how he can have a home at all; for of all blessings no gift equals the gentle, trusting, loving companionship of a good woman.

HAPPINESS & EQUALITY

I BELIEVE in the blessed trinity of Man, Woman, and Child. These to me express Divinity.

Happiness lies in equality. The woman should be the companion of the man, not his slave, pet, plaything, drudge, and scullion. The effort you put forth to win the woman, you should be compelled to exercise through life in order to hold her.

The house of the harlot exists because love is gyved, fettered, blindfolded, and sold in the market places. There is nothing so pulls on the heartstrings of the normal, healthy man as the love for wife and child. Always and forever he wears them in his heart of hearts.

In our hearts Divine Wisdom implanted the seeds of loyalty and right. These are a part of the great plan of self-preservation. We do not walk off the cliff, because we realize that to do so would mean death.

Make men and women free, and they will travel by the Eternal Guiding Stars.

That which makes for self-respect in men and women, putting each on their best behavior, increasing the sum of good-will and lessening hate, will have a most potent influence on future generations.

I can not imagine a worse handicap than to be tumbled into life by incompatible parents and be brought up in an atmosphere of strife. All that tends to tyranny in parents manifests itself in slavish traits in the children. Freedom is a condition of the mind, and the best way to secure it is to parent it.

The quality of the people turns on the quality of the parents; and especially does the quality of the child turn on the peace, happiness, and well-being of the mother. You can not make the mother a disgraced and taunted thing and expect the progeny to prosper.

> **A man who marries a woman to educate her falls a victim to the same fallacy as the woman who marries a man to reform him.**

A Marriage
of Minds

A CORRESPONDENT asks me this: "Do brilliant men prefer brilliant women?"

First, disclaiming the gentle assumption that I am brilliant, I say, yes.

The essence of marriage is companionship, and the woman you face across the coffee urn every morning for ninety-nine years must be both able to appreciate your jokes and to sympathize with your aspirations. If this is not so, the man will stray, or else chase the ghosts of dead hopes through the grave-yard of his dreams.

By brilliant men is meant, of course, men who have achieved brilliant things—who can write, paint, model, orate, plan, manage, devise, and execute.

Brilliant men are but ordinary men who, at intervals, are capable of brilliant performances. Not only are they ordinary most of the time, but often at times they are dull, perverse, prejudiced, and absurd.

So here is the truth: Your ordinary man who does the brilliant things would be ordinary all the time were it not for the fact that he is inspired by a woman.

Great thoughts and great deeds are the children of married minds.

When you find a great man playing a big part on life's stage, you'll find in sight, or just around the corner, a great woman. Read history!

A man alone is only half a man; it takes the two to make the whole.

Ideas are born of parents.

Now life never did, nor can, consist in doing brilliant things all day long.

Before breakfast most men are rogues. And even brilliant men are brilliant only two hours a day. These brilliant moments are exceptional. Life is life to everybody. We must eat, breathe, sleep, exercise, bathe, dress, and lace our shoes. We must be decent to folks, agreeable to friends, talk when we should, and be silent when we ought.

To be companionable—fit to live under the same roof with good people—consists neither in being pretty nor clever. It all hinges on the ability to serve. No man can love a woman long if she does not help him carry the burden of life. He will support her for a few weeks, or possibly years, then if she doesn't show a disposition and ability to support him, her stock drops below par. Men and women must go forward hand in hand. A brilliant man is dependent on a woman, and the greater he is the more he needs her.

The brilliant man wants a wife who is his friend, a companion to whom he can tell the things he knows, or guesses, or hopes; one with whom he can he can act out his nature. If she is stupid all the time, he will have to be brilliant, and this will kill them both.

Robert Louis, the Beloved, used to tell of something he called "Charm." But even his subtle pen, with all its witchery, could not quite describe charm of manner—that gracious personal quality which meets people, high or low, great or small, rich or poor and sends them away benefited, blessed and refreshed.

Ellen Terry, turned sixty, has it. She rests her chin in her hand and looks at you and listens in a way that captures, captivates, and brings again the pleasures of past years.

We are all just children in the Kindergarten of God, and we want playfellows.

If a woman is pretty, I would say it is no disadvantage, unless she is unable to forget it. But plainness of feature does not prohibit charm of manner, sincerity, honesty, and the ability to be a good housekeeper and a noble mother.

There are many degrees of brilliancy, but as a general proposition this holds: A brilliant man wants a wife who is intellectually on his wire—one who, when he rings up, responds.

This is Paradise!

THE WOMAN WHO UNDERSTANDS

EVERY man whose life and aspirations are touched with the Spirit spends his life, perhaps unconsciously, looking for the Ideal Woman—the woman whose soul will make good the deficiencies in his own.

He feels his weakness, his incompleteness; he is conscious that alone he is but half a man, but if he could only find Her—his other half—all would be as God designed it.

The Woman who Understands gives life and healing and complements the soul of a strong man.

WOMEN'S FREEDOM

THE position of woman as set forth in the Bible is one of slavery. The Pauline doctrine that women should learn in silence with all due subjection runs like a rotten thread through all the fabric of Christianity. And as the Second Commandment was the death of art for a thousand years ("Thou shalt not make unto thee any graven image, or any likeness of any thing that is in heaven above or earth beneath"), so has the forced servility of woman held our civilization in thrall to a degree that no man can compute.

The enslaving of women and holding them by law came in only when man was getting a bit "civilized." The pure, happy life of Nature would pale at the thought of abusing one's mate. Among wild animals, the females are protected: no tigress is ever abused or imposed upon—in fact, she would not stand it. In a condition of untrammeled Nature, animals are eminently just and moral in their love-affairs. In a state of captivity, however, they will sometimes do very unbecoming things.

> **Until men grant to women all the rights they demand for themselves, they will dwell in a spiritual Siberia.**

The flaunting boast that woman owes her freedom to the Christian religion is only advanced by ignorant and over-zealous people. Honest scholarship knows otherwise.

In the *Germania*, Tactus says that among the ancient Teutons the women were looked up to with a sort of sanctity. They were the mothers of men yet to be, and were treated with delicacy and deference; and in the state councils their advice was always listened to. Between the man and his wife there existed a noble comradeship.

In pagan Iceland, women were treated better than we treat them today. The Icelanders recognized their intelligence and were in full possession of the truth that the children of a man and a woman who are mental equals and who mutually respect and love each other, are far better than children born of slaves. To this end, where love had died, they freely granted divorce when both parties desired it, and in all ways they sought to strengthen and encourage marriages prompted by love.

Christianity accepted the idea of women's inferiority as a matter of course, emphasizing the strange delusion that "through woman's fault man fell." Thus woman was blamed for the evil of the world, and even little souls fresh from God were said to be born in sin.

The Jewish law required a woman to do penance and make sacrifice for her fault of bearing a child; all of which monstrous perversion of truth seems pitiable when compared with pagan Greece, where men uncovered their heads on meeting a woman with child and solemnly made way, feeling that they were in the sacred presence of the mystery of the Secret of Life.

PATRIARCHAL MARRIAGE: THE DEATH OF PASSION

AFTER marriage, men no longer win their wives; they own them. And women, living in the blighting atmosphere of a continuous personal contact that knows no respite, drift off into apathetic, dull indifference. The wife becomes an animal; the husband a brute. The lively grace, the tender solicitude, the glowing animation, the alert intellect, the sympathetic heart, the aspiring spirit—where are these now? They are gone—dead as the orange-buds that erstwhile opened their shell-like petals to catch the strains of the Wedding March—dead.

That men and women bring about their spiritual bankruptcy through gross ignorance, I have not the least doubt. And I am fully convinced that while woman has a sure and delicate insight into many things, in this particular she is simply ignorant and willful. The profound Doctor Charcot says, "I have known many men who endeavored to put their marital relations on a gentle, chivalric basis, but in nearly every case the wife interposed a tearful, beseeching veto, or else she filed a hot accusation of growing coldness that could only be disproved in one way. Virtuous women very seldom know anything of the psychology of love until it is too late to use the knowledge, and young women, thinking they know already, can not be taught."

Our modern custom of marriage is the doom of chivalry and death of passion. It wears all tender sentiment to a napless warp, and no wonder is it that the novelist hesitates to follow the couple beyond the church door.

FREEDOM & OBEDIENCE IN MARRIAGE

WOMEN should not "obey" men, any more than men should obey women; but the desire of the man and woman who are mentally and spiritually mated is to obey each other.

Obey? God help me! Yes, if I loved a woman, my whole heart's desire would be to obey her slightest wish. And how could I love her unless I had perfect confidence that she would only aspire to what was beautiful, true, and right? The only rivalry between us would be as to who could love most, and the desire to obey would be the one controlling impulse of our lives.

We gain freedom by giving it, and the one who bestows faith receives it back with interest. To bargain and stipulate in love is to lose.

Perfect faith implies perfect love; and perfect love casteth out fear. The price of a perfect love is an absolute surrender. To win all, we must give all.

Love, Human & Divine

WE would know nothing of love if we did not see it manifest in humanity, and the only reason we believe in the love of God is because we find love on earth.

The thought of the love of God can not be grasped in the slightest degree, even as a working hypothesis, by a person who does not know human love.

How else can we reach Heaven save through love? Who ever had a glimpse of the glories that lie beyond the golden portals save in loving moments?

Yes, this we know: all human handiwork that creates beauty in form has its rise in the loves of men and women. Love is vital, love is creative, love is creation. It is love that shapes the plastic clay into forms divinely fair. Love carves all statues, writes all poems, paints all the canvases that glorify the walls where color revels, sings all the songs that enchant our ears.

Without love, the world would only echo cries of pain, the sun would only shine to show us grief, each rustle of the wind among the leaves would be a sigh, and all the flowers fit only to garland graves.

Love—that curious life-stuff which holds within itself the spore of all mystic possibilities: that makes alive all dull wits, gives the coward heart, and warms into being the sodden senses: that gives joy and gratitude, and rest and peace: shall we not call thee God?

Do you say that I place too much importance on passion? I say to you that I have not sufficient imagination to exaggerate the importance of Love. It is as high as the heavens, as deep as hell, as sublime as the stars and great as the galaxy of worlds that fade on our feeble vision into mere Milky Ways. Love holds within her ample space all wrecks, all ruins, all grief, all tears; and all the smiles, and sunshine, and beauty that mortals know are each and all her priceless gifts, and hers alone.

> **Love goes to those who are deserving, not to those who set snares for it and lie in wait.**

THE POWER OF LOVE

It is a wonderful thing to have somebody believe in you. This is the great benefit of love.

Love idealizes its object. It exaggerates little tendencies into great virtues, possibilities into genius. Where much is expected from an individual, he may rise to the level of events and make the dream come true.

Mother-love is the great, surging, divine current that plays forever through humanity. We see it manifest in all animals; in the mother bird who dies rather than desert her young; in the tigress who is invincible when she has her babies to protect.

How much individuals of genius owe to their mothers will never be told in cold words, because love cannot be analyzed, nor placed under the slide.

LOVE & DEATH

The lover idealizes and clothes the beloved with virtues that exist only in his imagination. The beloved is consciously or unconsciously aware of this, and endeavors to fulfill the high idea; and in the contemplation of the transcendent qualities that his mind has created, the lover is raised to heights

> **Falling in love is the beginning of all wisdom, all sympathy, all compassion, all art, all religion; it is the one thing in life worth doing.**

otherwise impossible.

Should the beloved pass from this earth while such a condition of exaltation exists, the conception is indelibly impressed upon the soul, just as the last earthly view is said to be photographed upon the retina of the dead.

The highest earthly relationship is in its very essence fleeting, for men are fallible, and living in a world where the material wants jostle, and time and change play their ceaseless parts, gradual obliteration comes and disillusion enters. But the memory of a sweet affinity once fully possessed, and snapped by Fate at its supremest moment, can never die from out the heart. All other troubles are swallowed up in this; and if the individual is of too stern a fiber to be completely crushed into the dust, time will come bearing healing, and the memory of that once ideal condition will chant in his heart a perpetual eucharist. And I hope the world has passed forever from the nightmare of pity for the dead; they have ceased from their labors and are at rest.

But for the living, when death has entered and removed the best friend, Fate has done her worst.; the plummet has sounded the depths of grief, and thereafter nothing can inspire terror.

At one fell stroke all petty annoyances and corroding cares are sunk into nothingness. The memory of a love lives enshrined in undying amber. It affords a ballast against all the storms that blow, and although it lends an unutterable sadness, it imparts an unspeakable peace. Where there is this haunting memory of a great love lost, there are also forgiveness, charity, and sympathy that make the man brother to all who suffer and endure.

To have known an ideal friendship, and have it fade from your grasp and flee as a shadow before it is touched with the sordid breath of selfishness, or sullied by misunderstanding, is the highest good. The constant dwelling in sweet, sad recollection of the exalted virtues of the one that is gone, tends to crystallize these very virtues in the heart of him who meditates upon them.

LOVE FOR LOVE'S SAKE

WE gain the Kingdom of Heaven by having Heaven in our hearts.

We reach God through the love of one.

Love for love's sake—there is nothing better. It sweetens every act of life.

Love grows by giving. The love we give away is the only love we keep.

Insight, sympathy, faith, and knowledge are the results of love.

Love for love's sake.

II.

LEARNING

Practical Education : A Manifesto

1. Our education is never complete, and life and education should go hand in hand to the end.

2. By separating education from practical life, society has inculcated the vicious belief that education is one thing and life another.

3. Five hours of intelligently-directed work a day will supply ample board, lodging, and clothing to the adolescent student, male or female.

4. Five hours of manual labor will not only support the students, but it will add to their intellectual vigor and conduce to their better physical, mental, and spiritual development.

5. This work should be directly in the line of education, and a part of the school curriculum.

6. No effort of life need be pointless, but all effort should be useful in order to satisfy the consciousness.

7. Somebody must do the work of the world. There is a certain amount of work to do, and the reason some people have to labor from daylight until dark is because others never work at all.

8. To do a certain amount of manual labor every day, should be accounted a privilege to every normal man and woman.

9. No person should be overworked.

10. All should do some work.

11. To work intelligently is education.

12. To abstain from useful work in order to get an education, is to get an education of the wrong kind.

13. From fourteen years up, every normal individual can be self-supporting, and to be so is a God-given privilege, conducive to the best mental, moral, and spiritual development.

14. The method of examinations, in order to ascertain how much the pupil knows, does not reveal how much the

pupil knows, causes much misery, is conducive to hypocrisy, and is like pulling up the plant to examine its roots.

15. People who have too much leisure consume more than they should, and do not produce enough.

16. To go to school for four years, or six, is no proof of excellence; any more than to fail in an examination is proof of incompetence.

17. The giving of degrees and diplomas to people who have done no useful things is puerile and absurd, since degrees so obtained are no proof of competence, and tend to inflate the ego of the holder.

18. All degrees should be honorary, and be given for meritorious service to society—that is, for doing something useful for somebody.

TEACHING IN SEASON

TEACHING things out of season is a woeful waste of time. It is also a great consumer of nerve-force, for both pupil and teacher.

For instance, the English plan of having little boys of eight study Latin and Greek killed a lot of boys, and probably never helped a single one to shoulder life's burden and be a better man. Knowledge not used, like anything else not used, is objectionable and often dangerous.

Nature intends knowledge for service, not as an ornament or for purposes of bric-a-brac.

The awkward and bashful boy from the country—with mind slowly ripening in its rough husk, gathering gear as he goes, securing knowledge in order to use it, and by using it, making it absolutely his own, and gaining capacity for more—is the type that scores.

EDUCATION THAT WORKS

THE priestly plan of having one set of people do all the thinking, and another set all the work, is tragedy for both.

To quit the world of work in order to get an education is as bad as quitting the world of work and struggle in order to be "good." The tendency of the classical education is to unfit the youth for work. He gains knowledge in advance of his needs.

The boy of eighteen who enters college and graduates at twenty-two, when he comes home wants to run his father's business. Certainly he will not wash windows. He has knowledge, but no dexterity; he has learning, but no competence. He owns a kit of tools, but does not know how to use them. And now, if his father is rich, a place is made for him where he can do no damage, a genteel and honorable place, and he hypnotizes himself and deceives his friends with the fallacy that he is really doing something.

In the meantime, the plain and alert young man brought up in the business keeps the chimes on the barrel, otherwise it would busticate.

Use and acquaintance should go hand in hand. Skill must be applied. All great writers learned to write in just one way—by writing. To acquire the kit is absurd—get the tools one at a time as you need them.

College has just one thing to recommend it, and that is the change of environment that it affords the pupil. This is what does him good— new faces, new scenes, new ideas, new associations. The curriculum is nil—if it keeps the fledgling out of mischief it accomplishes its purpose.

But four years in college tends to ossification instead of fluidity—and seven years means the pupil gets caught and held by environment: he stays too long.

Alexander von Humboldt was right— one year in any college is enough for anyone. One year gives him inspiration and all the spirit of good there is in it; a longer period fixes frats, fads, and fancies in his noodle as necessities.

Happy is the one, like Ralph Waldo Emerson, who is discarded by his Alma Mater, or like Henry Thoreau, who discarded her.

In God's name, get weaned!

> **That person is the best educated who is the most useful.**

EDUCATION THROUGH EXPRESSION

THE education that aims at mere scholarly acquirement, rather than useful intelligence, will have to step down and out. The world needs competent people; then, if their hearts are right, culture will come as a matter of course.

We grow through expression—if you know things there is a strong desire to express them. It is Nature's way of deepening our impressions— this thing of recounting them. And happy, indeed, if you know a soul with whom you can converse at your best.

EDUCATION THROUGH TRAVEL

TRAVEL, as a means of broadening one's horizon, and giving a new point of view, has no substitute.

A human is a migratory animal. We learn by keeping in motion; by travel; by transplantation; in moments of joy and times of grief. Only running water is pure, and Sir Oliver Lodge says that a planet not in motion would dissolve into a gas and be lost.

Young men and women should be allowed to try their wings. The desire to "go somewhere" is natural and proper. Do not oppose it. Also, do not insist on a chaperone. If you travel with someone who looks up the route, keeps tab on the train, and buys the tickets, you lose, in great degree, the benefits of travel.

A youth of fifteen or sixteen who is allowed to go away a hundred miles or so on a visit, or on a business errand, will get more good out of the trip than they would get in a year at a boarding-school under the fussy care of a man with his collar buttoned behind, or brass buttons all up and down his martial front. We grow through making decisions.

The actual benefit of college does not come so much from curriculum as from the change of environment. New people, new scenes, new conditions with which to cope—these are the things that spur growth.

> Academic education is the act of memorizing things read in books and things told by college professors, who got their education by memorizing things read in books and told by college professors.

information, is the college the future will demand.

I do not know of a single college or university in the world that focuses on qualities, excepting Tuskegee Institute.

At Harvard, Yale, Dartmouth, Columbia, and Princeton, cigarette-smoking is so common that a stranger may suppose it compulsory. Professors teach the tobacco habit by example, and the boy who does not acquire the habit is regarded as eccentric.

At all our great colleges, exercise is limited to athletes. Instead of physical culture there are sports teams, and the students who need the gymnasium most are ashamed to be seen there.

How would the scientific cultivation of these qualities do?

Bodily Qualities—Health of digestion, circulation, breathing, manual skill, vocal speech, and ease in handling all muscles.

Mental Qualities—Careful thought, patience, decision, perseverance, courage, tact, concentration, insight, observation, accuracy, and memory.

Moral Qualities—Putting one's self in another's place, or thoughtfulness for

COLLEGE & CHARACTER

IT is the possession of qualities that fit a you for a life of usefulness, not the mental possession of facts. The school that best helps to form character, not the one that imparts the most others, which includes kindness, courtesy, good-cheer, honesty, fidelity to a promise, self-control, self-reliance, and self-respect.

THE SCHOOL OF LIFE

EDUCATION means growth, evolution—efficiency. That person is best educated who is most useful.

Some of the very strongest and most influential people who have ever lived never had the "advantages" of an academic education.

Of course it is equally true that great numbers of college graduates have gone on to success; but, on the other hand, a college degree is no proof of competence. Of the college men who succeed, who shall say they succeeded because of college, or in spite of it?

I would have everyone have a college education, in order that they might see how little the thing is really worth. I would have everyone rich, that they might know the worthlessness of riches.

To take young people away from work, around age eighteen, and keep them from useful labor for four years, in the name of education, will some day be regarded as a most absurd proposition.

Set in motion by theologians, the idea was that young people should be drilled and versed in "sacred" themes. Hence,

the dead languages and the thought that education should be esoteric.

This separation from the practical world for a number of years, where no useful work was done and the whole attention fixed on abstract themes and theories, often tended to cripple people so that they could never go back to the world of work and usefulness. They were no longer producers, and had to be supported by tithes and taxes.

And, of course, as they did not intend to go back to the world of work and usefulness, it really didn't make any difference if they did sink into a pupa-like condition of nullity.

Through travel we vitalize our ideas.

In the smaller colleges, many instances are found of students working their way through school. My experience leads me to believe that such students stand a very much better chance in the world's race than those who are made exempt from practical affairs by having everything provided. The responsibility of caring for one's self is a necessary factor in a person's evolution.

To make young people exempt from the practical world, from eighteen to twenty-two, is to run the risk of ruining them for life. Possibly you have taken opportunity from them , and turned them into mere memory machines.

There are persons who are always talking about preparing for life. The best way to prepare for life is to begin to live.

A school should not be a preparation; a school should be life.

Isolation from the world in order to prepare for the world's work is folly. You might as well take a boy out of the blacksmith-shop in order to teach him blacksmithing.

College is make-believe, and every college student knows it. From the age of fourteen upward pupils should feel that they are doing useful things, not merely killing time; and so their work and their instruction should go right along hand in hand.

The truly educated person is the useful one.

III.

LABOR

Worker's Creed

IBELIEVE in working, not weeping; in boosting, not knocking; and in the pleasure of my job. I believe that people get what they go after, that one deed done today is worth two deeds tomorrow, and that no one is down and out until he has lost faith in himself.

I believe in today and the work I am doing; in tomorrow and the work I hope to do, and in the sure reward which the future holds.

I believe in courtesy, in kindness, in generosity, in good-cheer, in friendship, and in honest competition. I believe there is something worth doing, somewhere, for everyone ready to do it. I believe I'm ready—right now!

Our business is to work—to surmount difficulties, to endure hardship, to solve problems, to overcome the inertia of our own nature, to turn chaos into cosmos by the aid of system—this is to live!

The Dignity of Labor

SAFETY lies in living like a pauper, no matter how much money you have. Bring your children up to be useful, to perform the necessary tasks of life, never to be above doing good, plain, old-fashioned work.

Any one who uses the term "menial" is touched with intellectualism. There are no menial tasks. The necessary is sacred, and the useful is divine.

Keep your feet on the earth, even though your head is in the clouds. Do not set yourself apart as something special and peculiar, with a high and lofty attitude. Have intellect, of course, but build it on a basis of common sense.

Robert Collyer was a blacksmith. Elihu Burritt was a shoemaker. Paul was a tentmaker. Jesus was a carpenter.

But now we have so separated things that, for the most part, carpenters and blacksmiths are excluded from "good society." How would a blacksmith look wearing white kid gloves at a reception?

Manual training is a necessary part of everyone's education. All should work with their hands. The trouble has been that we have given all the work to one set of people, and the culture to another set, and the result has been the degradation of both.

> **Be a creator, not merely a creature and a consumer.**

THE POVERTY
OF THE RICH

No greater shock ever comes to a young person from the country who makes his way up to the city, than the discovery that rich people are, for the most part, woefully ignorant. He has always imagined that material splendor and spiritual gifts go hand in hand; and now, if he is wise, he discovers that millionaires are too busy making money, and too anxious about what they have made, and their families are too intent on spending it, to ever acquire a calm, judicial, mental attitude.

The rich need education really more than the poor. "Lord, enlighten Thou the rich!" should be the prayer of everyone who works for progress. "Give clearness to their mental perceptions, awaken in them the receptive spirit, soften their callous hearts, and arouse their powers of reason."

Danger lies in their folly, not in their wisdom; their weakness is to be feared, not their strength. That the wealthy and influential class should fear change, and cling stubbornly to conservatism, is certainly to be expected. To convince this class that spiritual and temporal good can be improved upon by a more generous policy has been a task a thousand times greater than the inciting of the poor to riot.

It is easy to inspire the discontented to advocate for reform, but to arouse the rich, and carry truth home to the blindly prejudiced, is a different matter.

THE BASIS
OF BUSINESS

THE only way to make money is to render a service for humanity—to supply something that people want, or to carry things from where they are plentiful to where they are needed.

The person who confers the greatest service at the least expense is the one whom we will crown with honor and clothe with riches. A business operating by any other policy is running in high gear, straight for the cliff.

Success turns upon one's ability to produce the goods. A business built by bunkum beckons bankruptcy.

BUSINESS AS PUBLIC SERVICE

JOSIAH WEDGWOOD has been called the world's first modern businessman; that is, he was the first to introduce factory betterments and to pay special attention to the idea of beauty.

His factory was surrounded by ample space, so as to insure proper light and ventilation. Also, he had flowerbeds and an extensive garden, where many of his people worked at odd hours. Josiah Wedgewood gave prizes for the best gardens and for the most beautiful backyards; and this, please remember, was nearly a hundred years ago.

Unfortunately, the times were not ripe for Wedgewood's ideas as to factory building and factory surroundings; nevertheless, he left his mark upon the times.

One thing sure, he influenced profoundly another great businessman, Robert Owen who, in degree, followed the Wedgewood idea and endeavored to make his factory not only a place for manufacturing things, but a place where men and women would evolve and grow and become. Robert Owen's factory was also a school.

Wedgewood and Owen were businessmen, and never claimed to be anything else. But business is human service, and the good businessman today is essentially a public servant.

DO GOOD WORK

THE recipe for self-confidence is: Do good work.

When you have reached a point where your work gives you a great, quiet joy, then comes self-confidence. You are now well out on the road to mastership.

"Courage," says Emerson, "comes from having done the thing before."

Robert Louis Stevenson said, "I know what pleasure is, for I have done good work."

Those who do good work do not have to talk, apologize, or explain. Their work speaks.

And even though there be no one to appreciate it, the worker feels in it a great, quiet joy. You relax, smile, rest, fully intent on taking up your labors tomorrow and doing better than ever.

The highest reward that God gives us for good work, is the ability to do better work. Rest means rust.

SALVATION THROUGH ACTION

PHILOSOPHERS of the Far East have told us that our deliverance from the evils of life must come through the killing of desire. We reach Nirvana—rest—through nothingness.

But today, it has been realized by a vast number of the thinking people of the world that deliverance from discent and sorrow is to be had, not through ceasing to ask questions or to act, but by asking one more—"What can I do?"—and then doing it.

When you go to work, action removes the doubt that theory cannot solve.

The rushing winds purify the air; only running water is pure; and the holy ones, if there are such, are those who lose themselves in persistent, useful effort.

The saint is the one who keeps his word and is on time. By working for all, we secure the best results for self; and when we truly work for self, we work for all.

Humanity evolves as we awaken, ask questions, and act.

WORK, HEALTH, STUDY

HAPPINESS hinges on habits; because habits rule our lives. Our habits put us to bed and they get us up in the morning. They seat us at the table, and they set us to work.

There are three habits which, with but one condition added, will give you everything in the world worth having, and beyond which the imagination cannot conjure forth a single addition or improvement. These habits are the Work Habit, the Health Habit, and the Study Habit.

If you have these habits, and also have the love of a partner who has the same habits, you are in Paradise now and here, and so are they.

Work, Health, and Study, with Love added, are a solace for all the stings and arrows of outrageous fortune—a defense against all the storms that blow; for through their use you transmute sadness into mirth, trouble into ballast, pain into joy.

Do you still say that religion is needed?

Then I answer that Work, Health, Study, and Love constitute religion. Moreover, that any religion that leaves any of these out is not religion, but fetish.

Yet most religions, over the centuries, have pronounced sexual love an evil thing. They have proclaimed labor a curse. They have said that sickness is sent from God; and they have whipped and scorned the human body as something despicable, and thus have placed a handicap on health, and made the doctor a necessity. And they have said that mental attainment is a vain and frivolous thing, and that our reason is a lure to lead us on to the eternal loss of our soul's salvation.

Now we deny it all, and proclaim that these will bring you all the good there is: Work, Health, Study—Love!

Work means safety for yourself and service to humankind. Health means

> **Responsibilities gravitate to the one who can shoulder them.**

much happiness and potential power. Study means knowledge, equanimity, and the evolving mind. Love means all the rest!

WORK IS FOR THE WORKER

We become robust only through exercise, and every faculty of the mind and every attribute of the soul grows strong only as it is exercised. So you had better exercise only your highest and best, else you will give strength to habits or inclinations that may master you to your great disadvantage.

Work is for the worker, and work is a blessing. The Bible does not teach that—it teaches that work is a form of punishment, and only a very grim necessity at best. Even the New Testament is full of sympathy and condolences for the bearer of burdens and those who are heavy laden. There is much about looking forward to a sweet rest in Heaven, but not a word about getting on with your job. Heaven, to many, is a long rest, and no religion has ever pictured a paradise where happiness came through useful activity.

And where in Holy Writ do you find any statement of this patent truth—There is a certain amount of work to do in the world, and the reason some folks have to work from daylight to dark is because some other folks never work at all—?

A certain amount of work is very necessary to growth. Work is a blessing, not a curse, because through it we acquire strength—strength of mind and strength of body. To carry a responsibility gives a sense of power.

Those who have borne responsibility know how to carry it; with heads erect and the burden well adjusted to their shoulders, they move steadily forward.

Those who do not know better drag their burdens behind them with a rope.

Work is for the worker!

> ## Joyous are the busy; dissatisfied are the idle.

"BUSYNESS"

The word business was first used in the time of Chaucer to express contempt for people who were useful. The word was then spelled "busyness."

In those days the big rewards were given to those who devoted their lives to conspicuous waste and conspicuous leisure. The one who destroyed most was king by divine right, and everybody took his word for it.

Even today we find that if you would go in "good society" you had better not lift a trunk, sift ashes, sweep the sidewalk, or carry a hoe upon your shoulder.

SYSTEMS FOR SUCCESS

THE measure of success in business is the ability to organize.

The measure of a person's success in literature is the ability to organize ideas and reduce the use of the twenty-six letters of the alphabet to a system so as to express the most in the least space. The writer does not necessarily know more than the reader, but must organize facts and march truth in a phalanx.

In painting, your success hinges on your ability to organize colors and place them in the right relation to give a picture of the scene that is in your mind.

Oratory demands an orderly procession of words, phrases, and sentences to present an argument that can be understood by an average person.

Music is the selection and systematization of the sounds of Nature.

Science is the organization of the common knowledge of the common people.

In all of life, raw materials lie scattered about us. We are measured by our ability to select, reject, and organize.

INNOVATION VS. INERTIA

THERE is a common tendency to cling to old ways and methods. Every innovation has to fight for its life, and every good thing has been condemned in its day and generation.

Error once set in motion continues indefinitely, unless blocked by a stronger force, and old ways will always remain unless someone invents a new way and then lives and dies for it.

In the application of electricity, Edison had not only to discover methods whereby electricity could be utilized, but he had to commercialize the proposition and educate the world to its use. And when George Westinghouse invented the airbrake, his real task was to convince the railroad world of its value.

The reason many people oppose innovation is not that they hate progress, but that they love inertia.

FROM RESOURCES TO WEALTH

THE country that sells raw materials will always be poor, just as the farmer who sells corn, and not hogs, will never lift the mortgage. If you have a forest, and can work it up into tables, chairs, bookcases, and violins you will make a deal more money than if you sell firewood.

The United States has one-sixteenth the population of the world. But we have one-third the wealth of the world. Our wealth comes from the ability to combine coal and iron-ore; lumber and steel bolts; leather and shoe-strings; paint and glue; rubber and steel.

So we have supplied the world automobiles, shoes, farm implements, locomotives, engines, brass castings, machinery, and manufactured commodities in a million forms.

We take paper, glue, leather, copper, steel, and make a Kodak camera. The value of the raw materials that go to make a Kodak is, say, twenty cents. The consumer in South Africa, England, Japan, or Germany pays five dollars for the machine, and counts it a bargain.

It is brain that makes value.

Henry Ford sells steel, brass, leather, and wood properly coordinated, at fifty cents a pound. Thereby he is able to pay a minimum wage of five dollars a day to American workers. He does this with the aid of a manufacturing equipment unequalled in any European country. Henry Ford first supplies the home market, and then he has facilities to supply the foreign trade. And so today there are Ford agencies in every civilized country.

What America should sell is not raw material—we should sell our genius, our talent, our skill, our efficiency, our organizing ability.

> **Do your work with your whole heart and you will succeed. There is such little competition!**

ART & COMMERCE

ART follows in the wake of commerce, for without commerce there is neither surplus wealth nor leisure. The artist is paid from what is left after people have bought food and clothing; and the time to enjoy comes only after the struggle for existence.

WOMEN IN THE ECONOMY

WOMEN are adding greatly to the welfare of society. Woman is a natural economist and a conservator. She does not need patronage, and paternalism is a thing from which she has suffered much.

Let women fit themselves for the production of wealth, and wealth will be theirs. Every school now is putting in business courses. There are business colleges everywhere that are doing splendid and helpful work, fitting women for paying positions.

Factories, offices, and department stores are, in degree, pedagogic institutions. The world is not moving as fast as we would like, but it is certainly moving, and it is moving in the right direction.

THRIFT

THRIFT is the habit of spending less than you earn.

If you are a thrifty person, you are happy. When you are earning more than you spend, when you produce more than you consume, your life is a success, and you are filled with courage, animation, ambition, good-will. Then the world is beautiful, for the world is your view of the world, and when you are right with yourself, all's right with the world.

The habit of thrift proves your power to rule your own psychic self. You are captain of your soul. You are able to take care of yourself, and then out of the excess of your strength you produce a surplus.

Thus you are not only able to take care of yourself, but you are able to take care of some one else—of wife, child, father and mother, to lend a hand to sick people, old people, unfortunate people. This is to live.

Loving labor and thrift go hand in hand. A person who is not thrifty is a slave to circumstance. If you have no surplus saved up you are the plaything of chance, the pawn of circumstance, the slave of some one's caprice, a leaf in a storm. Fate says, "Do this or starve."

The surplus gives you the power to dictate terms, but most of all it gives you an inward consciousness that you are sufficient unto yourself.

Therefore, cultivate the habit of thrift, and the earlier you begin, the better. And no matter how old you are, or how long you have lived, begin this day to save something, no matter how little, out of your earnings.

> To have worked is to have succeeded—we leave the results to time. Life is too short to gather the harvest — we can only sow.

SUCCESS BY NATURE

SUCCESS is the most natural thing in the world. The individual who does not succeed has placed himself in opposition to the laws of the universe.

The world needs you—it wants what you produce. If you can serve it, and if you will, it will reward you richly.

By doing your work, you are moving in the line of least resistance. You need what others have to give—and they need you. To reciprocate is wisdom. To rebel is folly.

To consume and not produce is a grave mistake, and upon such a one Nature will visit her displeasure.

Success demands concentration—oneness of aim and desire. Those who can lose themselves in their work are the ones who will succeed best.

Courtesy, kindness, and concentration—this trinity forms the "open sesame" that will unlock all doors.

IV.

CREED

My Creed

I BELIEVE in the Motherhood of God. I believe in the blessed Trinity of Father, Mother and Child.

I believe that God is here, and that we are as near Him now as ever we shall be. I do not believe He started this world a-going and went away and left it to run itself.

I believe in the sacredness of the human body, this transient dwelling-place of a living soul, and so I deem it the duty of every man and every woman to keep his or her body beautiful through right thinking and right living.

I believe that the love of man for woman, and the love of woman for man, is holy; and that human love in all its promptings is as much an emanation of the Divine Spirit as love for God, or the most daring hazards of the human mind.

I believe in salvation through economic, social, and spiritual freedom.

I believe John Ruskin, William Morris, Henry Thoreau, Walt Whitman, and Leo Tolstoy to be prophets of God who rank in mental reach and spiritual insight with Elijah, Hosea, Ezekiel, and Isaiah.

I believe that people are inspired today as much as they ever were.

I believe we are now living in Eternity as much as ever we shall.

I believe that the best way to prepare for a future life is to be kind, live one day at a time, and do the work you can do the best, doing it as well as you can.

I believe we should remember the weekday to keep it holy.

I believe there is no devil but fear.

I believe that no one can harm you but yourself.

I believe in my own divinity—and yours.

I believe that we are all children of God, and it doth not yet appear what we shall be.

I believe the only way we can reach the Kingdom of Heaven is to have the Kingdom of Heaven in our hearts.

I believe in everyone minding their own business.

I believe in freedom—social, economic, domestic, political, mental, spiritual.

I believe in sunshine, fresh air, friendship, calm sleep, beautiful thoughts.

I believe in the paradox of success through failure.

I believe in the purifying process of sorrow, and I believe that death is a manifestation of life.

I believe the universe is planned for good.

I believe it is possible that I shall make other creeds, and change this one, or add to it, from time to time as new light may come to me.

WE ARE ONE

HUMANITY! I wonder what a person really is! Starting from a single cell, this seized upon by another, and out of the Eternal comes a particle of the Divine Energy that makes these cells its home.

Growth follows, cell is added to cell, and there develops a human being—a person whose body, two-thirds water, can be emptied by a single dagger-thrust and the spirit given back to its Maker in a moment.

My heart goes out to you, o human, because I can not conceive of any being greater, nobler, more heroic, more tenderly loving, loyal, unselfish, and enduring than you are. All the love I know is human love. All the forgiveness I know is human forgiveness. All the sympathy I know is human sympathy.

And hence I address myself to humanity—to you—and you I would serve. The fact that you are a human being brings you near to me. It is the bond that unites us. I understand you because you are a part of myself. You may like me, or not—it makes no difference. If ever you need my help I am with you.

Often we can help each other most by leaving each other alone; At other times we need the hand-grasp and the word of cheer. I am only a man—a mere man—but in times of loneliness think of me as one who loves his kind. What your condition is in life will not prejudice me either for or against you.

What you have done or not done will not weigh in the scale. If you have been wise and prudent I congratulate you— unless you are unable to forget how wise and good you are, and then I pity you.

If you have stumbled and fallen and been mired in the mud, and have failed to be a friend to yourself, then you of all people need friendship, and I am your friend.

I am the friend of convicts, insane people, and fools—successful and unsuccessful, college-bred and illiterate. You all belong to my church.

I could not exclude you if I would. But if I should shut you out, I would then close the door upon myself and be a prisoner indeed.

The spirit of friendship that flows through me, and of which I am a part, is your portion, too. The human race is one, and we trace to a common Divine ancestry.

WHAT IS THE SOUL?

THE mind sees, hears, listens, sifts, weighs and decides.

Over against this, there is something in us that sees the mind and watches its workings—which analyzes the mind and knows why it does certain things.

And this something is the soul.

The soul is the highest conception of excellence and truth we can bring forth. And from seeing what one soul is, we imagine what all souls may be—and thus we reach God, who is the Universal Soul.

THE RELIGION OF HUMANITY

THE old and once popular view of life that regarded a human being as a sinful, lost, fallen, despised, despicable and damned thing has very natu-rally tended to kill in us enthusiasm, health, and self-reliance. Probably it has shortened the average length of life more than a score of years.

When people come to realize that they are part and particle of the Divine Energy that lives in all they see and feel and hear, they will, indeed, be in a position to claim and receive their birth-right. And this birthright is to be healthy and happy.

The Religion of Humanity does not seek to placate the wrath of a non-resident deity, nor does it worship an absentee god. It knows nothing of gods, ghosts, goblins, sprites, fairies, devils or witches. I would not know a god if I saw one coming down the street in an automobile.

If ever a man existed who had but one parent, this fact of his agamogen-esis would not be any recommendation to us, nor would it make special claim on our reverence and regard. Rather, it would place him outside of our realm, so that what he might do or say would not be vital to us. He would be a differ-ent being from us, therefore his experi-ences would not be an example for us to follow.

The Religion of Humanity knows nothing of a vicarious atonement, jus-tification by faith, miraculous concep-tion, transubstantiation, original sin, Hell, Heaven, or the efficacy of baptism as a saving ordinance.

It does not know whether a person

lives again as an individual after death or not.

It is not so much interested in knowing whether a book is "inspired" as whether it is true.

It does not limit the number of saviors of the human race, but believes that any man or woman who makes this world a better place is in degree a savior of humankind. It knows that the world is not yet saved from ignorance, superstition and incompetence, nor redeemed from a belief in miracles. And hence it believes that there must be saviors yet to come.

It believes that the supernatural is the natural not yet understood.

The Religion of Humanity is essentially monistic—it believes that there is but one thing in the world. This one thing has been called by many names: the Divine Energy, the Universal Intelligence, the First Principle, and "God." This One Thing has a million myriad manifestations. It incarnates itself as gas, as matter, as vegetation, as animal-life. Its highest manifestation, to my knowledge, is humanity.

If you were asked what a human being is, the definition would be: a human being is a transient, thinking, conscious, reasoning, and sometimes unreasonable manifestation of Divine Energy.

> **If all Christians were like Christ, there would be no need for Christianity.**

But humanity is not yet fully created—we are only in process. When you read history and find from what distance we have come, and see what tremendous progress has been made, one thinks of the future possibilities of humanity with reverence and awe.

And the part we now play, as forerunners and messiahs of the coming humanity, is to summon all our sense of sublimity, all our love, all our heroism, all our devotion.

We have ceased to look upon humanity with scorn and suspicion; ceased to calumniate and libel our kind by calling us worms of the dust, born in sin and conceived in iniquity; ceased to drone that pitiable untruth, "There is no health in us" (*The Book of Common Prayer*, Morning Prayer); ceased to disparage human reason; ceased to talk about "bodily pleasures" and "worldliness" as if to enjoy life and do the world's work were base, sinful, and wrong.

To devote ourselves to the service of humankind, and to realize that we can help ourselves only by helping others, this is the Religion of Humanity. By and through this religion we attain health, happiness, and prosperity, here and now.

We eliminate fear, sickness, and poverty only as we cease to break Nature's laws, and by recognizing and having faith in the Supreme Intelligence of which we are a part. This Intelligence is a form of motion—it is Energy—and we as parts of it are successful just in the degree that we move with it.

Sanity consists in service. When we work for others, we benefit ourselves.

Wisdom is the distilled essence of intuition, corroborated by experience. And Wisdom tells us that life, and life in abundance, lies only in work, love, laughter. And when I use the word work, I mean work with head, heart, and hand.

A Religion of Kindness

A RELIGION of just being kind would be a pretty good religion—don't you think so?

We used to think it was people's beliefs concerning a dogma that would fix their place in eternity. This was because we believed that God was a grumpy, grouchy old gentleman, stupid, touchy and dictatorial. A really good man would not damn you, even if you didn't like him; but a bad man would.

As our ideas of God changed, we ourselves changed for the better. Or, as we thought better of ourselves, we thought better of God.

It will be character that locates our place in another world, if there is one, just as it is our character that fixes our place here. We are weaving character every day, and the way to weave the best character is to be kind and to be useful.

Think right, act right; it is what we think and do that makes us what we are.

Evolving Beliefs

FROM being regarded as The Book, the Bible is now looked upon as one of many books, and is only worthy of respect as it instructs and inspires. We read it with the same reverence that we read Emerson and Whitman.

The preacher was once a commanding figure in every community. Now he is regarded as a sort of poor relation. The term "spiritual adviser" is only a pleasantry. We go to the businessman for advice, not the priest. If a book is listed on the *Index Librorum Prohibitorum*, all good Catholics read it in order to know how bad it is.

Those who institute heresy trials have no power to punish—they only advertise.

Christianity was evolved, as all religions have been—it was not inspired. It grew in a natural way and it declined by the same token. Whether it has benefited the human race is a question which we need not discuss now. That it ministered to poverty and disease is true, and that it often created the ills which it professed to cure is equally a fact.

Poverty, ignorance, repression, superstition, coercion, and disease, with nights of horror and days of fear, are slinking away into the past; and they have slunk further and further away the more Christianity's clutch upon the throat of the race has been loosened.

The night is past—the day is at hand! The East is all aglow! Health, happiness, freedom, and joy are all calling to us to arise and sing our hymn to labor. Our prayer is, "Give us this day our daily work, and we will earn our daily bread."

Our religion is one of humanity. Our desire is to serve. We know that we can help ourselves only as we help others, and that the love we give away is the only love we keep.

We have no fears of the future, for we have no reason to believe that the Power which cares for us in this life will ever desert us in another.

EVOLVING PEOPLE

ALL the justice we know is human justice. That which we call God's justice is only a person's idea of what they would do if they were God; this idea changes as humanity changes; and humankind's conception of God's justice has softened, refined, and become less severe than ever before.

And all the love we know is human love. And all compassion, human compassion; and all sympathy, human sympathy; and all forgiveness, human forgiveness.

There is nothing finer, greater or nobler in the world than humanity.

All beings, spirits, and persons greater than human beings have been, and are, the creation of the human mind.

All laws, creeds and dogmas are of only transient value, and should be eliminated when they no longer minister to human happiness.

Now, for the first time in the history of the world, a very large number of people know these things. They are exercising their brains, and the brain is an organ that grows strong only through use.

Humanity is not yet completed, but only in process of creation; and humankind has not yet attained full control of its intellect. Our ability to think is a new acquisition; very few people as yet are able to think at all, being driven by hunger, fear, and the hope of reward.

To be scientific, one must be able to classify and coordinate the facts that logic and reason supply; and to be philosophic, one must be able to unify and deduce right conclusions from science.

Philosophic thinking gives wings to the imagination. This faculty is only in its infancy. Through right thinking, we will gradually learn to control our bodies, our tempers, our desires, and our environment.

The trained imagination is a searchlight which reveals the future, and by the use of imagination we now see Paradise ahead. A Paradise of increasing effort, work, endeavor, and increasing power; a Paradise of this world that is to come through health, work, simplicity, honesty, mutuality, cooperation, reciprocity, and love.

LIVE NOW AND HERE

THAT is good which serves men and women—this earth is the place, and the time is now. To live now and here the best one can is the finest preparation for any life to come.

We no longer accept the doctrine that our natures are rooted in infamy, and that the desires of the flesh are cunning traps set by Satan, with God's permission, to undo us. We believe that no one can harm us but ourselves, that sin is misdirected energy, that there is no devil but fear, and that the universe is planned for good.

On every side, we find beauty and excellence held in the balance of things. We know that work is a blessing, that Winter is as necessary as Summer, that night is as useful as day, that death is a manifestation of life, and just as good.

We believe in the Now and Here. We believe in humanity, and we believe in a power in ourselves that makes for righteousness.

These things have not been taught us by a "superior class" who govern us and to whom we pay taxes and tithes—we have simply thought things out for ourselves. We have listened to Coleridge, Emerson, Brisbane, Charles Ferguson, and others, who said: "You should use your reason and separate the good from the bad, the false from the true, the useless from the useful. Be yourself and think for yourself; and while your conclusions may not be infallible they will be nearer right than the conclusions forced upon you by those who have a personal interest in keeping you in ignorance.

"You grow through exercise of your faculties, and if you do not reason now you will never advance. We are all sons and daughters of God, and it doth not yet appear what we shall be. Claim your heritage!"

> Don't worry about getting safely out of this world and into Heaven. To live fully, here and now, is the problem—one world at a time is enough.

REDEEMING PAST MISTAKES

MAKING people live in three worlds at once—past, present, and future—has been the chief harm organized religion has done. To drag your past behind you, and look forward to sweet rest in Heaven, is to spread the present very thin.

The person who lives in the present, forgetful of the past and indifferent to the future, is the person of wisdom.

If you have made mistakes in the past, reparation lies not in regrets, but in thankfulness that you now know better.

It is true that we are punished by our sins, and not for them; it is true also that we are blessed and benefitted by our sins. Having tasted the bitterness of error, we can avoid it. If we have withheld the kind word and the look of sympathy in the past, we can today give doubly, and thus, in degree, redeem the past. And we best redeem the past by forgetting it and losing ourselves in useful work.

It is a great privilege to live. Thank God! There is one indisputable fact: We are here!

SALVATION

Do not be disturbed about saving your soul—it will be saved if you make it worth saving.

Do your work. Think the good. And evil, which is a negative condition, shall be swallowed up by good. Think no evil; and if you think only the good, you will think no evil.

Life is a search for power. To have power you must have life, and life in abundance. And life in abundance comes only through great love.

The age is crying for humanity—civilization wants people who can save it from dissolution; and those who can benefit it most are those who are freest from prejudice, hate, revenge, whim, and fear.

Two thousand years ago lived one who saw the absurdity of loving only his friends—he saw that this meant faction; lines of social cleavage, with ultimate discord; and so he painted the truth large and declared that we should love our enemies and do good to those who despise us.

It is not necessary for us to leave our tasks and pattern our lives after his, but if we can imitate his sublime patience and keep thoughts of discord out of our lives, we, too, can work such wonders that it will truthfully be said that we are sons and daughters of God.

There isn't much rivalry here—be patient, generous, and kind, even to foolish folk and absurd people. Be one with all—be universal. So little competition is there in this line that anyone, in any walk of life, who puts jealousy, hate, and fear behind will become distinguished.

Do this, and all good things shall be yours.

DAMNATION

Christianity supplies a Hell for the people who disagree with you and a Heaven for your friends.

The distinguishing feature of Christianity is the hypothesis that humanity is born in sin and conceived in iniquity; that through Adam's fall we sinned all; and to save us from eternal death and damnation, the Son of God died on the cross, and this Son was God, Himself.

These things are still in its creeds and confessions of faith. Has the Roman Catholic Church or any of the orthodox Protestant churches officially repudiated its creed, and made a new one founded on industry, reciprocity, sweetness, and light?

Human beings are the only creatures in the animal kingdom that sit in judgment on the work of the Creator and find it bad—including Nature and humanity itself.

God, we are told, looked upon His work and called it good; this is where the clergy of Christendom take issue with Him.

No greater insult was ever offered to God than the claim that His chief product, humanity, is base at heart and merits damnation.

> **We are not punished *for* our sins, but *by* them.**

THE WORLD IS GETTING BETTER

WITH the past twenty-five years, sensible people have abandoned the idea of hell, and a personal devil is now only a huge joke.

"Spare the rod and spoil the child," was once considered a great and vital truth, but now we spare the rod and save the child. Love, patience, and kindness are answering the purpose much better than the rod.

Capital punishment has been done away with in some states, and will be a thing of the past before long. To kill the murderer, we find, neither brings the victim back to life, nor does it prevent other crimes. The time will most assuredly come when jails and penitentiaries will have to go, as well.

The best lawyers now keep people out of trouble instead of getting them in. The best doctors no longer simply treat symptoms—they seek the cause and tell you the truth. The best preachers acknowledge they do not know anything about another world, and they preach social salvation here and now.

The world is growing better. That many people behold the chimera of "respectability through conspicuous waste," and are refusing to conform their lives to it, is very hopeful. Conspicuous waste and conspicuous leisure do not bring health, happiness, long life, nor contentment.

Once we thought work was a curse; then it came to us that it was a necessary evil; and yesterday the truth dawned upon us that it is a blessed privilege. There is joy in useful effort.

We want to do what is best for ourselves, and we have made the discovery that what is best for ourselves is also best for others.

FROM DARKNESS TO LIGHT

THE old idea that we love darkness rather than light is a libel on humanity and a denial of the wisdom and goodness of the Supreme Intelligence.

When certain unmarried men, who had lost their capacity to sin, sat indoors, breathing bad air, and passed resolutions about what was right and what wrong, making rules for the guidance of the people instead of trusting the natural, happy instincts of the individual, they ushered in the Dark Ages. These are the gentlemen who blocked human evolution absolutely for a thousand years. They dethroned the Universal Intelligence and set up a theocracy founded on bad air, indigestion, and fear.

And yet, in absolute fairness, the fact that there were prehistoric races that have vanished and left no successors, like the mound-builders, the cliff-dwellers, and the Aztecs, gives ground for reasoning that these people were self-destroyed, through failure to adjust themselves to the Divine Economy. Then there are the civilizations that once existed in Egypt, Assyria, Greece, and Rome, which were destroyed by a failure to obey the divine law, but which, in dying, like a rotting log that nourishes a bank of violets, supplied us with rich legacies of truth and beauty.

After all her seeming failures, Nature, or the Universal Energy—or God, if you please—persistently keeps on filling the hearts of all people with a desire for perfection, so that today millions are studying the history of the nations gone, in order that we may avoid the pitfalls of the past. This is proof in itself that the heart of humanity is right.

> **Theologians dogmatize because the burden of proof is on the opposition. We have to die to find out whether they are right.**

HOLY BOOKS

A TRAVELER reports that, in Africa, a general sent a written message to his lieutenant a hundred miles away. After the lieutenant had looked at the flimsy little piece of paper, behold! he knew just where his chief was and how it fared with him—and this without the messengers saying a word. Then, the messengers who carried the little piece of paper fall down on their faces in awe and fear before the lieutenant.

In Mexico, I have been in villages where only one man—the priest—could read and write, and it was not hard to imagine why the people of the place looked upon the priest as the agent of Deity, the mouthpiece of God.

Even in America, when the rumble of printing-presses never dies from our ears, the newspaper editorial carries a certain specific gravity and is quoted as authority, when the spoken words of the man himself are scarcely listened to, certainly not remembered, even by his barber.

It was not so very long ago that a book bound in oaken boards, riveted in bands of iron wrought in curious shapes, locked with ponderous key, born upon a silver salver by a stoled and tonsured priest of God, was carried in solemn processional with silent steps and slow to the altar. Then the book was unlocked, opened, and from it the priest chanted in strange, unknown tongue, and the people listened in breathless awe to the words that Deity had dictated in order that men might be saved from an impending doom.

Families have been severed, churches divided, cities separated into factions, aye, nations destroyed—all through a difference of opinion as to whether or not certain literary works were directly communicated by God.

"In times of old all books were religious oracles. As literature advanced, they became venerable preceptors; they then descended to the rank of instructive friends; and as their number increased, they sunk still lower—to that of entertaining companions."

There is truth in these words of Coleridge, but books have not sunk; rather, people have been raised to a degree where they are the companions of the authors who instruct and entertain them.

No longer do we crawl with our faces in the dust before a tome.

THE FOLLY OF THEOLOGY

IT has been said that Luther set back civilization by a thousand years. He prolonged the life of theology by presenting it in a palatable capsule, just at a time when intelligent humanity was making wry faces, getting ready to spew it out.

The rancor of priests and popes in opposition to Luther only elevated him into a world-power and made possible a thousand warring, jarring, quibbling sects and systems, consuming one another and wasting the time and substance of humankind in their vacuous theological antics.

Theology starts with an assumption and ends in a fog.

Nobody ever understood it, but vast numbers have pretended to because they thought others did. Very slowly we have grown honest, and now wise and good men accept the doctrine of the unknowable.

Theology was not meant to be understood, but to be believed.

A theologian is an ink-fish you can never catch. And in stating this fact, I fully appreciate that I am laying myself open to the charge of being a theologian, too.

THE UNKNOWABLE

METAPHYSICS reaches its highest stage when it affirms, "All is One" and "All is Mind." But this does not long satisfy, and we begin to ask, "What is this One? What is Mind?"

The highest wisdom lies in knowing that we do not know anything, and never can, concerning a First Cause. The laws of Nature do not account for the origin of the laws of Nature. All we find is phenomena, and behind phenomena, phenomena.

The bitterness of theology toward science arises from the fact that, as we find things out, we dispense with the arbitrary god, and his business agent, the priest.

So far as we can judge, the unknown cause that rules the world by unchanging laws is moving forward to happiness, growth, justice, peace, and right. Therefore, the scientist, who perceives that all is good when rightly received and rightly understood, is really the priest and holy man—the mediator and explainer of the mysterious.

The person of faith is the one who discards all thought of "how it first happened." Fix your mind on the fact that you are here. The more we study the conditions that surround us, the greater our faith in the truth that all is well.

All progress in mind, body and material things has come to humanity through the study of cause and effect. And just in degree as we abandoned the study of theology as futile and absurd, and centered on helping ourselves here and now, have we prospered.

The more we know of this world the better we think of it, and the better we are able to use it for our advancement.

THE KNOWABLE

IN courts of law, the phrase "I believe" has no standing. Never a witness gives testimony but that they are cautioned thus: "Tell us what you know, not what you believe."

In theology, belief has always been regarded as more important than that which your senses say is so. Almost without exception, a "belief" is a legacy, an importation—something borrowed, an echo, and often an echo of an echo.

The Creed of the Future will begin, "I know," not "I believe." And this creed will not be forced upon the people. It will carry with it no coercion, no blackmail, no promise of an eternal life of idleness and ease if you accept it, and no threat of hell if you don't.

It will have no paid, professional priesthood, claiming honors, rebates and exemptions, nor will it hold estates free from taxation. It will not organize itself into a system, marry itself to the state, and call on the police for support. It will be so reasonable, so in the line of self-preservation, that no sane man or woman will reject it, and when we really begin to live it we will cease to talk about it.

CHILDISH EXPLANATIONS

EXPLANATIONS are made for other people. Parents answer children, not by telling them the actual truth, but by giving them an explanation that will satisfy—one that they can mentally digest. To say, "the fairies brought it," may be all right until a child begins to ask who the fairies are, and wants to be shown one, and then we have to make the somewhat humiliating confession that there are no fairies.

This mild fabrication, in reference to Santa Claus and the fairies, is right and proper mental food for children. Their minds can not grasp the truth that some things are unknowable; and they are not sufficiently skilled in the things of the world to become interested in them scientifically—they must have a resting-place for their thoughts, and so the fairy-tale comes in as an aid to the growing imagination.

But we place no penalty in disbelief in fairies, nor do we make offers of reward to all who believe that fairies actually exist. Neither do we tell children that people who believe in fairies are good, and that those who do not are wicked and perverse.

The fairy-tale and theological stages may be necessary, but the sooner we are graduated out of them the better.

THE BENEFITS OF SIN

SWIMMING uneasily in my ink-bottle is an essay on the benefits and advantages of Sin.

As yet I do not feel myself competent to fish it out. I am waiting, hoping that some one else will do the task for me. It is a delicate and elusive bit of work, and no matter how well done, I know that the one who does it will lay himself open to the charge of being an advocate of the Devil.

Yet the fact remains that Sin has in very many instances led the way to sainthood. It is the Magdalene, who from out of the purging fires of purgatory completes the circle and arises pure and spotless, recognizes Deity incarnate when all others blindly fail.

There is something startling in the truth that the woman who preserves her "virtue" pays a price for the privilege.

There is even a penalty in achieving success. Where is the preacher who dares face the fact that the "honest" man or woman with fixed income, happily situated, is to a degree isolated from all sympathy and fellowship with the great mass of beings who suffer and endure the slings and arrows of outrageous fortune?

People are great only as they possess sympathy, and that which causes you to center on yourself and your own attainments—whether worldly or spiritual—oblivious to the struggles of others, is not, cannot be, wholly good.

Through sin do we reach the light, and that which teaches us cannot be wholly bad.

> **The supernatural is the natural not yet understood.**

THE SONG OF SONGS

In one of Mr. Spurgeon's sermons he says, "Holy Writ exists for the purpose of showing man his duty to God." The Song of Songs, however, is peculiar in that it is one the two books in the Bible that contains no reference to a Supreme Being.

In this poem, a man belonging to the Chosen People is talking with a woman who is a heathen; and if this couple know anything of God they keep the knowledge strictly to themselves.

The man makes no effort to convert the woman; indeed, she seems fully as intelligent as he: not a hint of Elohim, or angels, or spirits, or devils, or heaven or hell; of man's duty to God, or man's duty to man; not a single moral injunction, not an ethical precept; not a suggestion of miracle is given, or of things supernatural—nothing but the earth and the beauty that is seen in it.

And yet the canonicity of the book has never been challenged save by a few captious critics of no standing in scholarship. The Holy Fathers could be cited at great length to show the high esteem and exalted reverence in which the Song has ever been held.

In the Mishna, Rabbi Akiba says: "Peace and mercy! No man in Israel ever doubted the canonicity of the Song of Songs, for the course of ages can not vie with the day on which the Song of Songs was given to Israel. All the Scriptures are indeed holy, but the Song of Songs is the Holy of Holies."

According to the statement of Luther, the Song is an allegory representing Solomon's relation to the Commonwealth of Israel. On the other hand, DeWitt Talmage was wont to explain that the Song is a prophetic parable referring to Christ as the bridegroom and the Church as the bride. Indeed, I believe this is the universal Evangelistic belief.

Long ago, Theodoret stated his

belief that the Song of Songs was simply a love dialogue which passed between Solomon and a certain Shulamite maiden. But to this a clamorous denial has rung down the centuries, and the assertion has repeatedly been put forward that mere love songs are not lovely things at all, and without some deep, hidden meaning in the lines the Song would not have been preserved, either by Divine Providence or the Wise Men of Old.

We today, however, perhaps swinging back to a view which corresponds with that of the author of the lines, do not regard passionate love as an unholy thing.

To me the Song of Songs is simply the purring of a healthy young man to a sun-kissed shepherdess, and she, tender hearted, innocent, and loving, purrs back, as sun-kissed maidens ever have and I suppose ever will.

This poem was composed, we have good reason to believe, fully three thousand years ago, yet its impressionistic picture of the ecstasy of youthful love is as charming and fresh as the color of a Titian.

An out-of-door love, under the trees, where "the beams of our house are cedar, and our rafters of fir, and our bed is green," is the dream of all lovers and poets. Thus the story of Adam and Eve in the Garden of Eden, "naked and unashamed," has been told a score of times, and holds its place in all Sacred Writ.

Shakespeare shows the idea in *As You Like It* and *The Tempest. Paul and Virginia* gives us a glimpse of the same thought; so does the *Emilé* of Rousseau; and more than once Browning suggests it in his matchless poems. Stevenson has touched deftly on the beautiful dream, as have other modern poets and storytellers.

Surely the love of man and woman is not an ungodly thing—else why should God have made it?

RATIONAL JUDAISM

IT is the belief now, among thinking people, that Moses, when he led the Children of Israel out of captivity, was not a religious fanatic, but a pragmatist. Moses did the thing he could do. He managed his people in the only way he could manage them. He did for them what was best; and the Mosaic Code is a sanitary code. It is a code for the here and now. It is a mode of living, and it is the sensible mode.

The Judaic Religion was a commonsense religion. It has passed through periods of fanaticism, but again, at this writing, for the most part, it has emerged out into the clear sunlight of reason. Rational Judaism is a universal religion, and its cornerstone is common sense.

A Prayer of Gratitude

I AM thankful for the blessed light of this day, and I am thankful for all the days that have gone before.

I thank the thinkers, the poets, the painters, the sculptors, the singers, the publishers, the inventors, the business-men, who have lived and are now living.

I thank Pericles and Phidias, who made the most beautiful city the world has ever seen, and were repaid by persecution and death.

I thank Aristotle, the mountain-guide and schoolteacher, who knew how to set bad boys to work.

I thank Emerson for brooking the displeasure of his Alma Mater.

I thank James Watt, the Scotch boy who watched his mother's tea-kettle to a purpose.

I thank Volta and Galvani, who fixed their names, as did Watt, in the science that lightens labor and carries the burdens that once bowed human backs.

I thank Benjamin Franklin for his spirit of mirth, his persistency, his patience, his commonsense.

I thank Alexander Humboldt and his brother, William Humboldt, those great brothers twain, who knew that life is opportunity.

I thank Shakespeare for running away from Stratford and holding horses at a theater-entrance—but not forever.

I thank Arkwright, Hargreaves, Crompton, from whose brains leaped the looms that weave with tireless hands the weft and warp that human bodies wear.

I thank Thomas Jefferson for writing the Declaration of Independence, for founding a public-school system, for dreaming of a college where girls and boys would study, learn, and work in joy.

I thank Baruch Spinoza, gardener, lensmaker, scientist, humanist, for being true to the dictates of the tides of divinity that played through his soul.

I thank Charles Darwin and Herbert Spencer, Englishmen, for liberating theology from superstition.

I thank Tyndall the Irishman, Draper the American, Herschel the German, Bjornson the Scandinavian, and Adam Smith the Scotchman, for inspiration and help untold.

These and others like them, their names less known, have made the world a fit dwelling-place for liberty. Their graves are mounds from which flares Freedom's torch.

And I thank and praise, too, the simple, honest, unpretentious millions who have worked, struggled, toiled, carrying heavy burdens, often paid in ingratitude, spurned, misunderstood—

> **A creed is a fossilized metaphor.**

who still worked on and succeeded, or failed, robbed of recognition and the results of their toil.

To all these who sleep in forgotten graves, my heart goes out in gratitude over the years and the centuries and the ages that have passed.

Amen, and Amen!

TEN POSITIVE COMMANDMENTS

I. Thou shalt think well of thyself and well of thy neighbor.

II. Thou shalt add to the health, wealth, and happiness of the world.

III. Thou shalt be on good terms with sunshine, fresh air, and water.

IV. Thou shalt get eight hours' sleep a day.

V. Thou shalt eat moderately, and exercise every day in the open air.

VI. Thou shalt love the memory of thy mother, and be true to the friends that have done so much for thee.

VII. Thou shalt recognize the divinity in all persons.

VIII. Thou shalt remember the weekday to keep it holy.

IX. Thou shalt remember that thou can only help thyself by helping other people, and that to injure another is to injure thyself, and that to love and benefit others is to live long and well.

X. Thou shalt love the stars, the ocean, the forest, and reverence all living things, recognizing that the source of life is one.

A PRAYER TO RADIATE LIFE

THE supreme prayer of my heart is not to be learned, rich, famous, powerful, or even good, but simply to be radiant. I desire to radiate health, cheerfulness, calm courage, and goodwill.

I wish to live without hate, whim, jealousy, envy, fear. I wish to be simple, honest, frank, natural, clean in mind and clean in body, unaffected—to say "I do not know," if it be so, and to meet all people with an absolute equality, to face any obstacle, and meet every difficulty unabashed and unafraid.

I wish others to live their lives, too, up to their highest, fullest, and best. To that end I pray that I may never meddle, interfere, dictate, give advice that is not wanted, or assist when my services are not needed. And if I can uplift or inspire, let it be by example, inference, and suggestion, rather than by injunction and dictation. That is to say, I desire to be radiant—to radiate life!

V.

COUNTRY

SHRINES OF LIBERTY

Every day in the year in come pilgrims to Mount Vernon—dozens, hundreds, thousands—and the interest in the place and its memories never fades.

At Monticello we tread softly over the green turf once pressed by the feet of Thomas Jefferson, who said, "That country is governed best that is governed least."

In a quaint little church at Richmond we are shown the pew where Patrick Henry stood when he exclaimed, "Give me liberty or give me death."

We make quest to Independence Hall, Philadelphia; and at Arch and Third Streets we look through the iron pickets on the grave of Benjamin Franklin.

On Boylston Street in Boston we read the name on a simple slab, "Sam Adams," and our hearts go out in admiration for the pamphleteer.

On Rector Street, in New York, just off busy Broadway, is a marble marked, "Alexander Hamilton," and every day hundreds remove their hats as they pass.

Then we go to Concord to visit Sleepy Hollow, where rests the dust of Ralph Waldo Emerson.

Not long ago I was in Spencer County, Indiana, down near the Ohio River, and visited a little village barely more than a railroad-station, and walked a half-mile up a hillside to a grave at the top of this hill, for here sleeps Nancy Hanks, mother of Abraham Lincoln.

Then we go to Springfield, Illinois, and pay silent tribute to Abraham Lincoln, Liberator of Humanity. And we realize that the name and fame of Lincoln grow brighter as the years go by.

Sometimes the place of pilgrimage is a battleground, at other times a church, or a house, more often a grave.

And the only places that are sacred shrines are where certain people have lived, worked, spoken, and died. And the theme of these people has always been one and the same, and that theme is Liberty.

No name lives enshrined in the hearts of humanity save the names of those who have fought Freedom's fight.

On the tombs of a few of these we carve simply one word—Savior. These are the ones who died that we might live. They flung away their lives for a noble cause, and that the only cause worth living for, fighting for, striving for, dying for—the cause of Freedom.

And we say with the orator: "I know not what discoveries, what inventions, what thoughts may leap from the brain of the world. I know not what garments of glory may be woven for the years to come. I can not dream of the victories to be won on the fields of thought; but I do know that coming from out the infinite sea of the future there will never touch this bank and shoal of time a richer gift, a rarer blessing, than liberty for man, woman, and child."

FRANKLIN

BENJAMIN FRANKLIN was the strongest all-round man that America has produced.

He was laborer, printer, business-man, inventor, scientist, publisher, financier, diplomat, philosopher. Every-thing Franklin touched he flavored with love and enthusiasm. Courage in his heart never died.

He had wit and humor, and humor is the sense of values. He knew a big thing from a little thing. He was able to laugh at life, and he sympathized with those who had failed or stumbled.

If ever a person saw the future illumined by the flame of a great and living imagination, it was Benjamin Franklin.

Three countries honored him. He borrowed money from France when America had no credit, and with this money Washington fought the battles of the Revolution. If anyone can be named who gave us freedom, it is Benjamin Franklin. He gave us freedom from superstition, from fear and doubt, woe and want. His plea was always and forever for industry, for economy. He prized the fleeting hours, and life to him was a precious privilege.

SACAJAWEA

IN the Lewis and Clark Expedition, there were thirty-four men and one woman.

This woman, Sacajawea, was the chief guide and counselor of Lewis and Clark. She knew the fords, passes, and springs; and when food was scarce she went alone to the Indian villages, where she was given food for herself and the men.

For two thousand miles she led the

way a-foot, her baby on her back. When hope sank in the hearts of the men she cheered them forward.

In Portland, Oregon, the white women of the land have erected a statue of this brave Indian woman. The artist has been singularly happy in his modeling—silent, sober, patient, firmly poised, she looks out wistfully to the western mountains and points the way. On her back is her pappoose, chubby and content, innocent of the thought that he is making history.

This noble bronze reveals the honest wife, the loving mother, the faithful friend, the unerring guide. Thousands looking upon this statue have been hushed into silence and tears. There is an earnestness in it that rebukes frivolity and inspires reverence.

JOHN BROWN

THERE is only one thing worth living for, writing for, working for, dying for—and that is freedom.

On the way to the gallows, a mother held up her baby boy, and John Brown stopped long enough to kiss the cheek of the little black baby.

To be kissed by a man who was on the way to the Ferry, going because he tried to make men free, is no small matter. It has been denied that John Brown kissed the black baby, but I reckon, that it was so, for I've seen that painting depicting the scene, by dear Tom Hovenden, who died rescuing a child from in front of a moving train.

John Brown was a fanatic, certainly, that is true. His methods were wrong, but the man himself was right, as every man is who lifts up his voice for freedom, and flings away his life that others may have liberty.

The path of progress is a winding, thorny road, and all along it one can trace the tracks of bleeding feet.

> We gain freedom by giving it. To enslave another is to enslave yourself.

THOREAU

HENRY DAVID THOREAU's place in the common heart of humanity grows firmer and more secure as the seasons pass, and his life proves for us again the paradoxical fact, that the only people who really succeed are those who fail.

Thoreau's obscurity, his poverty, his lack of public recognition in life, either as a writer or as a lecturer, his rejection as a lover, his failure in business, and his early death form a combination of calamities that make him as immortal as a martyr. These things array us on the side of the man against unkind fate, and cement our sympathy and love.

In Sleepy Hollow Cemetery at Concord there is a monument marking a row of mounds where half a dozen Thoreaus rest. The inscriptions are all of one size, but the name of one Thoreau alone lives, and he lives because he had thoughts and expressed them for the people.

YELLOWSTONE

THERE is just one objection to Yellowstone Park, and that is that it exhausts your supply of adjectives.

Usually we describe things by saying they are like this or they remind you of that. But Yellowstone Park reminds you of things you have seen and experienced only in dim eons past and ages gone.

You look upon the gushing geysers, the towering crystal peaks, the dashing streams, the limpid lakes, the mountains lifting themselves to the skies, cold, solemn and imperturbable, and your eyes turn at last to the eternal blue overhead, and you are hushed, awed, subdued, and the sense of sublimity holds you fast. Tears come as a great relief.

No one can ever describe Yellowstone Park, because what you see and feel there is beyond compare, and therefore beyond speech. You feel there as did Leonardo when he tried to portray the face of his lady-love.

You see Niagara Falls and you go away and talk about it; you see Yellowstone Park and you go away and think about it. It is an experience, and never again are you quite the same person. You have been close to Infinity.

Robert Browning tells us of Lazarus, who, having come back from the confines of death, could not speak of what he had seen, because there was nobody he could talk with who had had a similar experience.

The person who has been to Yellowstone Park can only talk about it with those who, too, have seen, known, and felt.

THE BUSINESS OF WAR & THE ART OF PEACE

ANYTHING you prepare for, you get. Nations that prepare for war will find an excuse for fighting.

The Law of Compensation never rests. There was no such thing as civilization until individuals ceased carrying arms, and agreed to refer their differences to the courts.

If Ohio and Pennsylvania have a misunderstanding, they do not go at it tooth and nail to destroy property—they have agreed on a way to adjust their misunderstandings.

The good sense of the world says today that nations should mediate and arbitrate.

The Warlord spirit is an anachronism. And no matter what it was once, today it is a detestable thing.

War preparedness leads to war.

The coastline between Canada and the United States, from the Saint Lawrence River to Lake Superior, is about two thousand miles. In the year Eighteen Hundred Twelve, there were forty-six forts, big and little, on the United States side, and about the same number frowned at us from Canada.

At Fort Niagara alone there were at one time six thousand troops. Altogether we had on the Great Lakes over a hundred craft devoted to the art of fighting—this in the interest of peace.

In one little battle we had with our British cousins on Lake Erie, Commodore Perry, a rash youth of twenty-seven, captured six British ships and killed three hundred men. A little before this, the British destroyed ten of our ships and killed two hundred Americans.

After the War of Eighteen Hundred Twelve was ended and peace was declared, both sides got busy, very busy strengthening the forts and building warships.

At Watertown, Conneaut, Erie, Port Huron, Cleveland, and Detroit were shipyards where hundreds of men were working night and day building warships. Not that war was imminent, but the statesmen of the time said there was nothing like "preparedness." In Canada, things were much the same.

> **The person who does not know how to follow orders is not fit to give them to others.**

Suddenly, but very quietly, two men in Washington got together and made an agreement. One man was acting Secretary of State, Richard Rush of Philadelphia; the other was Charles Bagot, Minister to the United States from England.

Rush was of Quaker parentage, and naturally was opposed to the business of war. Bagot had seen enough of fighting to know that it was neither glorious nor amusing.

Rush wrote out a memorandum of agreement which he headed "An Arrangement." The document is written on one side of a single sheet of paper and is dated April twenty-eight, Eighteen Hundred Seventeen. Here is a copy:

"1. The Naval Forces henceforth to be maintained upon the Great Lakes shall be confined to the following vessels on each side.

"2. On Lake Ontario one vessel, not to exceed one hundred tons burden, carrying not more than twenty men and one eighteen pound cannon.

"3. On the Upper Lakes two vessels, of same burden, and armed in a like way.

"4. On Lake Champlain one vessel of like size and armament.

"5. All other armed vessels to be at once dismantled, and no other vessel of war shall be built or armed along the Saint Lawrence River or on the Great Lakes."

This agreement has been religiously kept. Its effect was to stop work at once on the fortifications, and cause disarmament along the Great Lakes.

So far as we know, the agreement will continue for all time. Both parties are satisfied, and in fact so naturally has it been accepted very few people know of its existence.

Here is an example that our friends in Europe might well ponder over. If those forts on the frontier had been maintained, and had the ships of war continued to sail up and down, it would have been a positive miracle if there had not been fighting.

Probably they would have forced us into a war with England before this. We have had several disputes with Canada when it would have been very easy to open hostilities if the tools had been handy. Those who tote pistols find reasons for using them, and the nations that have big armies will find excuse for testing their efficiency.

If two countries can make an "arrangement" limiting the extent of armament, and this arrangement holds for a hundred years, can not nine countries do the same? Then all that is needed is a few soldiers to do police duty.

America is a giant; it is well to have a giant's strength but not well to use it like a giant. This is the richest country the world has ever known—in treasure and in men and women. If we mind our own business and devote our energies to the arts of peace we can solve a problem that has vexed the world from the beginning of time.

Leave Us Alone!

IT is safe to say that, in civilized countries, ninety-nine people out of a hundred are opposed to war.

We are farmers, mechanics, merchants, manufacturers, teachers, and all we ask is the privilege of attending to our own business. We own our homes, love our friends, are devoted to our families, and do not interfere with our neighbors any more than is necessary.

We have work to do, and wish to work while it is day. We recognize that life is short, and the night cometh. Leave us alone!

But they will not—these demagogues, politicians, and rogues intent on the "strenuous life." We wish to be peaceable and want to be kind, but they say this life is warfare and we must fight.

Of course we would fight to protect our homes; but our homes are not threatened, nor our liberties, save by those who insist on the strenuous life. Leave us alone!

We wish to pay off the mortgages on our houses, to educate our children, to work, to read, to meditate, to prepare for old age and death. But they will not leave us alone, these men who insist on governing us and living off our labor. They tax us, eat our substance, conscript us, draft our boys into their wars to fight farmers whose chief offenses are that they cultivate an objectionable style of whisker and wear trousers that bag at the knee.

They deceive us—this ruling class—they hoodwink us; they betray us; they bulldoze us by the plea of "patriotism."

They deceive us in the name of the bleeding Christ—the gentle Christ whose love embraced a world—the Christ who distinctly taught us that war is wrong, and that the only rule of life should be to do unto others as we would be done by. Oh, the infamy and shame of it!

Pretending to follow in the footsteps of Christ, they call themselves Christians. Comparatively few people think for themselves, and so this deception acts as a hypnosis upon the many, and—though being peaceably disposed—they accept it.

The Bible is a book often talked about, but seldom read. Christ never endorsed war. Not even a war of self-defense, much less a war of aggression. Christ never took up a collection, accepted no salary, founded no church, had no ritual, wore no mitre nor robe

> **The recipe for perpetual ignorance is: Be satisfied with your opinions and content with your knowledge.**

of office. He did not belong to the ruling class—did not even take pains to associate with respectable people. He was a carpenter who felt certain truths so intensely that he left his bench for a time and went forth speaking to people in the streets, the market places, and by the seashore.

Christ taught humility, meekness, the forgiveness of one's enemies, and that to kill is wrong. The Bible teaches us not to swear oaths, but the ruling class swears on the Bible in which they do not believe.

So the people who wish to follow the teachings of Christ are not allowed to do so, but are taxed, outraged, deceived—by the ruling class who demand that we shall lead the strenuous life, when all we ask is the privilege of doing our work—and doing unto others as we would be done by.

The plain people of all nations are opposed to war. We only wish to be let alone. Men with wives, children, sweethearts, homes, aged parents, horses, cattle, crops, and flowers, do not want to go off and fight someone. We are peaceable and wish to be kind. War is hell. We hate it.

We would like to obey the Golden Rule, but the ruling class will not have it so—they pass conscription laws, and use the army thus conscripted to conscript other men.

War is the sure result of the existence of armed men. That country which maintains a large standing army will sooner or later have a war on hand. The man who prides himself on fisticuffs is going, some day, to meet a man who considers himself a better man, and they will fight.

Force expends itself and dies. Every army is marching to its death; the aggressor is overcome by the poison of his pride; victory is only another name for defeat—but the spirit of gentleness and of love is eternal. Only by building on that can we hope as a nation to live.

We wish to do our work. We wish to beautify our homes, to educate our children, to love our neighbors.

Leave us alone!

Your false cry of danger and "Wolf! Wolf!" shall not alarm us. We pay your war taxes of a million dollars a day only because we have to, and we will pay no more and no longer than we have to.

The only relief lies in education. We will educate people into the thought that the life of peace and goodwill is better than the strenuous life of strife, bloodshed, and war. We will defy the ruling class by refusing to bow down to their religion of bullets.

"Peace on Earth"—it can only come when nations do away with armies, and are willing to do unto others as they would be done by.

Leave us alone!

WHY I AM AN ANARCHIST

AN Anarchist is one who minds his own business. An Anarchist does not believe in sending warships across wide oceans to kill brown people, and lay waste to rice fields, and burn the homes of people fighting for liberty.

Destruction, violence, ravages, murder, are perpetuated by statute law. Without law, there would be no infernal machines, no war ships, no dynamite guns, no flat-nosed bullets, no pointed cartridges, no bayonets, no policeman's billies, no night sticks, no handcuffs, no strait-jackets, no dark cells, no gallows, no prison walls to conceal the infamies therein inflicted. Without law, no little souls fresh from God would be branded "illegitimate", indelibly, as soon as they reach Earth.

Europe is divided up between eight great governments, and in time of peace over three million men are taken from the ranks of industry and are under arms, not to protect the people, but to protect one government from another.

I do not believe in governing by force, or threat, or any other form of coercion. I would not arouse in the heart of any of God's creatures a thought of fear, or discord, or hate, or revenge. I will influence people, if I can, only by aiding them to think for themselves; so they, of their own accord, may choose the better part—the ways that lead to life and light.

I do not believe in bolts or bars or brutality. I make my appeal to the Divinity in all, and they, in some mysterious way, feeling this, do not fail me. I send valuable books without question, upon postal-card request, to every part of the Earth where the mail can carry them, and my confidence is never abused. The Roycroft Shop is never locked, employees and visitors come and go at pleasure, and nothing is molested. My library is for anyone who cares to use it.

I fix my thought on the good that is in every soul and make my appeal to that. And the plan is a wise one, judged by results. It secures you loyal helpers, worthy friends, gets the work done, aids digestion, and brings sound sleep at night.

Unjust Laws

Any law that can be easily broken is a bad law. Any tendency in life that is wrong, which is palliated and perpetuated by society, is unethical.

Everyone is agreed that we should make it easy for everybody to do what is right, and difficult to do what is wrong. That is, we should reward, by a natural automatic process, everything which tends to human betterment; and we should discourage, by withholding a reward, everything which tends to double-dealing, falsity, finesse, chicanery.

> **People are great only as they are kind.**

Law is one thing and justice is another.

We think of how the greatest men and women in history have been berated, reviled, imprisoned, and their property confiscated; and if they lived long enough, they were executed, and the public was given a holiday.

We think of how Pericles, who built the city of Athens, was destroyed and disgraced, and how he had to go in the Forum and plead for the life of his wife, Aspasia.

We think of how the son of Pericles and Aspasia was executed on order of the government.

We think of how Phidias, the right hand of Pericles, and the greatest sculptor the world has ever seen, was executed for blasphemy on account of having put the picture of his patron on a sacred shield, how he was dragged at the cart's tail to the place of execution, and his body thrown to the wild beasts.

We think of how Socrates, the greatest mind, perhaps, the world has ever known, was passed the deadly hemlock on order of a jury of five hundred who sat on his case.

Surely, Socrates could not complain that he did not have a fair trial. He had his day in court, and his passing, written by his pupil, Plato, is one of the immortal things in literature.

The glory that was Greece lingers around the lives of Socrates, Aspasia,

Pericles, Phidias, Herodotus, Hippocrates, and Aristotle—all criminals before the law—all disgraced, exiled or executed.

Greek history lives but for these, and the men most instrumental in destroying them live only, if at all, because they linked their names with greatness.

ELECTING A MESSIAH

HERBERT SPENCER deals at length with what he is pleased to term the "Messianic Idea." It seems that all nations have ever held the hope of the coming of a Strong Man, who would deliver them from the ills that beset their lives. This hope never dies, although it assumes different forms varying according to conditions.

No doubt that the hope that springs eternal in the United States, when each four years roll round, is a rudimentary survival of the Messianic Idea. As yet, however, the president who is to take the bitterness out of this cup of life has not been elected.

NEW WORLDS
TO CONQUER

IN history there are three people who conquered the world: Alexander, Caesar, and Napoleon. Their method of conquering was through violence. They had no desire to give themselves to the world; they were intent on honors, ease, luxury, and lust for power.

Today, we see a milky way of new worlds to conquer. These worlds yet unconquered are economic, political, pedagogic, philosophic, artistic and scientific.

The University Militant is now engaged in fighting:

1. For the rights of women.

2. For the rights of children.

3. For the rights of criminals.

4. For the rights of all animals.

5. To make all work and business beautiful.

6. For the elimination of theological fetish—a thing that has caused more misery and bloodshed than all other causes combined.

7. For the elimination of medical superstition, to the end that humankind shall be freed from racial fear, one of the most prolific causes of insanity and disease.

8. For the eradication of parasitism, through the reformation of our social ideals and our systems of education, so that every man and woman shall know the joys of earning an honest living.

9. Against the tyranny of fashion as applied to clothes, housekeeping and social customs.

10. For the disarmament of the nations, and international arbitration.

All the world we should attempt to conquer is our own world.

Also, it is well to remember what Aristotle told Alexander: that the greatest dangers that confront an army are not in the ranks of the enemy, but are in its own camp. That is to say, our greatest enemies are those which lurk in our own hearts—hate, fear, jealousy, sloth, greed, inertia, appetite.

Choose your division and enlist in the army that is fighting for human rights. Don't be a neutral—get in the fight and stand back to the wall.

Be one of a glorious minority. Be a Greek, and never let yourself be swallowed up by a Persian mob. Dare to stand alone, to fight alone, to live alone, to die alone! Otherwise you will not live at all—you will only exist.

VI.

CHARACTER

HABITS CREATE CHARACTER

Only character counts. And what is character?

Well, first, character is a matter of habits. The young man or woman who, working all day in a shop or factory, will get a certain amount of outdoor exercise and then buckle down to some course of intellectual improvement for one hour out of the twenty-four, is going to become a distinguished person.

But to slide, glide, drift, loll, dawdle, with no definite objective point in mind, is to arrive at the point of Nowhere and to have your craft lie hopelessly becalmed on Mud Flats.

Walk in the open air, dig in the garden, play ball, then buckle down to an hour at the lessons, and you are bound to be a winner.

Life is complex, difficult. The struggle exists as it never has before. We need all the equipment we can get. But in spite of numbers, opportunities were never so great as they are today.

There is no such thing as complete success. After every achievement comes the voice, "Arise, and get thee hence, for this is not thy rest!"

So we never arrive, but always we work, we struggle, we strive, and this continual endeavor is all there is of life.

But when life is methodized, when we work, study, play, and laugh, flavoring all with love, we have found the key to the situation.

MAKE MOTION EQUAL EMOTION

The secret which I am about to impart is the most valuable and far-reaching of any known to humanity.

It is the key to health, happiness, wealth, power, success. It is the "open sesame" to Paradise, here and now.

A secret is something known only to a few. Often the best way to retain a secret is to let others help you to keep it. The only way to retain love is to give it away—art and religion the same.

So here, then, is the secret: Let Motion equal Emotion.

Must I elucidate? Very well, I will: There is only one thing in the world, and that is Energy. This Energy takes a myriad million forms; and its one peculiarity is that it is always in motion.

In Nature there is nothing inanimate. Everything is alive; everything is going somewhere, or else coming back; nothing is static. Fixity is the one impossible thing.

And the fallacy of fixity has been the one fatal error of theology and all philosophies in the past. Progress consists in getting away from the idea of the static.

Nature's one business is to absorb and to dissipate—to attract and repel—to take in and give out. And everything which Nature makes is engaged in the same business.

A human takes in carbon and gives off nitrogen. The plant takes in nitrogen and gives off carbon. All things are in motion, ebb and flow, action and reaction, cause and effect, swirl and whirl. Centripetal and centrifugal forces make our life on the planet Earth possible.

That which we call static is merely equilibrium. The heart rests between beats. The tiger crouches for one of two reasons: to spring or to die.

And death is a form of life. Death is a combination where the balance is lost, and gas, water, and solids are in wrong proportions. The only thing then is to dissolve the body and use in new masses the substances that composed it.

MAKE ACTION EQUAL ENERGY

HUMAN beings are transformers of energy. This energy plays through us. In degree we can control it; or at least we can control our condition as transmitters. And the secret of being a good transmitter is to allow motion to equal emotion.

To be healthy and sane and well and happy, you must do real work with your hands as well as with your head. The cure for grief is motion.

The recipe for strength is action. To have a body that is free from disease and toxins, you must let motion equal emotion.

Love with no outlet creates a current so hot that it blows out the fuse. But love that finds form in music, sculpture, painting, poetry, and work is divine and beneficent beyond words.

That is, love is an inward emotion, and if stifled, thwarted, and turned back upon itself, tends to gloom, melancholy, brooding, jealousy, rage, and death.

But love that is liberated in human efforts attracts love; so a current is created and excess emotion is utilized, for the good not only of the beloved, but also of the human race.

The love that lasts is a trinity. "I love you because you love the things that I love." Static love soon turns to hate, or, to be more exact, try to make love a fixity and it dies.

Safety lies in service. Going the same way, we will go hand in hand.

A lover out of a job is a good man for a girl to avoid.

Religion that takes the form of ecstasy, with no outlet in the way of work, is dangerous. This way horror lies. Emotion without motion tends to madness and despair.

MAKE EXPRESSION EQUAL IMPRESSION

EXPRESSION must equal impression. If you study, you must also create, write, teach, give out. Otherwise, you will become a plaster-of-Paris cat or a brass monkey. If great joy has come to you, pass it along, and thus do you double it. You are the steward of any gift the gods have given you, and you answer for their use with your life. Do

> **Character is the result of two things: mental attitude and the way we spend our time.**

not obstruct the divine current. Use your knowledge and use it quickly, or it will disintegrate and putrefy.

The school where the child learns, and then goes home and tells what he has learned, approaches the ideal. On the other hand, the college that imparts knowledge but supplies no opportunity for work is faulty in the extreme. A school for adults that does not supply work as well as facts is false in theory and vicious in practice. Its pupils do not possess health, happiness, or power, except on a fluke.

Emotion balanced by motion eliminates dead tissue and preserves sanity. For lack of motion, congestion follows.

Most sickness comes from a failure to make motion balance emotion. Impress and express; inhale and exhale; work and play; study and laugh; love and labor; exercise and rest. Study your own case and decide to get the most out of life.

The education of invalids is a terrific waste. Sickness, unhappiness, ignorance, all tend to inefficiency.

Realize that you are a Divine Transformer. Make motion equal emotion, and you will eliminate fear and be efficient to the last. And to live long and well is to accept life in every phase—even death itself—and find it good.

INDUSTRY, CONCENTRATION & SELF-RELIANCE

IT is not the attainment of knowledge that marks the superior person—it is the possession of certain qualities.

There are three traits of character, or habits, or personal qualities, which once attained, mean money in the bank, friends at court, honor and peace at home.

These qualities are Industry, Concentration, and Self-Reliance.

The individual who has these three qualities is in possession of the key that unlocks the coffers of the world. All doors fly open at his touch. "Oh, he's a lucky dog," they say—and he is.

And the strange part of it is, there is no mystery about the acquirement of these three things; no rites nor ritual; you do not have to memorize this or that, nor ride a goat; the secret of these qualities is not locked up in dead languages; no college can impart them, and the university graduates who fail, fail for lack of them.

On the other hand, no one ever succeeded beyond the average who did not possess them. And it is an indictment of our colleges and universities when we consider the fact that the people who have these qualities usually acquired them at "The University of Hard Knocks"—and in spite of parents, guardians, teachers, and friends.

Let us take three great Americans and see what made them supremely great: Washington, Jefferson, Franklin.

Let a certain quality stand for each man: Washington (Self-Reliance); Jefferson (Concentration); Franklin (Industry).

> **When habits are young, they are like lion cubs. They grow day by day. Eventually they rule you.**

But each of these men had all three of these qualities, and without these qualities the world would never have heard of them, and without these three men, America today would not be known as a Nation.

It was only the self-reliance of Washington at Valley Forge which saved independence from being "a lost hope." Washington was hooted and denounced for preferring starvation to defeat, but the persistence of the man never faltered. It was a losing fight for most of those long, dragging, dread, nine years—a fight against great odds—poverty against wealth, farmers against trained troops, barracks against the wind-swept open. But Washington believed in his cause and best of all he believed in himself.

"It is only a question of which side gets discouraged first. I know we will outlast them. Give in? Never! This fight is mine." You can't whip a man who talks like that. And as time went by, George the Third had brains enough to sense it, Cornwallis felt it, all England began to acknowledge it, and best of all America knew it.

It wasn't fighting that won the independence of the Colonies: it was the generalship and self-reliance of George Washington. This self-reliance shaped his actions, and finally spread over the land. Our political blessings, as a people, come to us through the unrelenting self-reliance of Washington.

INITIATIVE

THE world bestows its big prizes, both in money and in honors, for but one thing.

And that is Initiative.

What is Initiative?

I'll tell you: It is doing the right thing without being told.

But next to doing the right thing without being told is to do it when you are told once.

Next, there are those who never do a thing until they are told twice: such get no honors and small pay.

Next, there are those who do the right thing only when Necessity kicks them from behind, and these get indifference instead of honors and a pittance for pay. This kind spends most of its time polishing a bench with a hard-luck story.

Then, still lower down in the scale than this, we find the fellow who will not do the right thing even when some one goes along to show him how, and stays to see that he does it: he is always out of a job, and receives the contempt he deserves, unless he has a rich father, in which case Destiny patiently awaits around the corner with a stuffed club.

To which class do you belong?

GENIUS

GENIUS is only the power of making continuous efforts. The line between failure and success is so fine that we scarcely know when we pass it: so fine that we are often on the line and do not know it.

How many people have thrown up their hands at a time when a little more effort, a little more patience, would have achieved success. As the tide goes clear out, so it comes clear in. In business, sometimes, prospects may seem darkest when really they are on the turn. A little more persistence, a little more effort, and what seemed hopeless failure may turn to glorious success.

There is no failure except in no longer trying. There is no defeat except from within, no really insurmountable barrier save our own inherent weakness of purpose.

SYMPATHY

No one is great who does not possess Sympathy.

Sympathy and Imagination are twin sisters. Your heart must go out to all: the high, the low, the rich, the poor, the learned, the unlearned, the good, the bad, the wise and the foolish; it is necessary to be one with them all, else you can never comprehend them.

Sympathy!—it is the touchstone to every secret, the key to all knowledge, the "open sesame" of all hearts. We all do what we do because we, at the time, think it is the best thing for us to do. Put yourself in the other person's place, and then you will know why he or she thinks certain things and does certain deeds.

Wise people do not blame. They may pity, but they do not attempt to punish, for they know that the law of consequences sees that exact justice is done and they never make the mistake of supposing that they are divinely appointed to act the part of a section of the day of judgment.

They will influence if they can—they will reform, educate, and lead out, but they will not repress or chastise.

Their lives will be one long pardon, one infinite love, and, therefore, one infinite strength.

The saviors of the world have simply been those with wondrous Sympathy.

THE ABILITY TO SAY NO

Individuals are strong just in proportion as they have the ability to say NO, and stand by it.

Look back on your own life—what was it that caused you the most worry, wear, vexation, loss, and pain? Wasn't it because you failed to say NO at certain times and stick to it?

This vice of the inability to say NO comes from lack of confidence in yourself. You think too much of the opinions of other people, and not enough of your own. And the real fact is that the good opinion of the best people comes from your saying NO, and not weakly yielding to a contract that doesn't benefit you.

Cultivate self-confidence and learn to say NO. It is a great thing to be a human, but it is a finer thing to be a master—master of yourself.

YOU ARE WHAT YOU THINK

Whenever you go out of doors, draw the chin in, carry the crown of the head high, and fill the lungs to the utmost; drink in the sunshine; greet your friends with a smile, and put soul into every handshake.

Do not fear being misunderstood; and never waste a minute thinking about your enemies. Fix firmly in your mind what you would like to do, and then you will move straight to the goal.

Keep your mind on the great and splendid things you would like to do; and then, as the days go gliding by you will find yourself unconsciously seizing upon the opportunities that are required for the fulfillment of your desire.

Picture in your mind the able, earnest, useful person you desire to be, and the thought you hold is hourly transforming you into that particular individual.

Thought is supreme. Preserve a right mental attitude—the attitude of courage, frankness, and good-cheer. To think rightly is to create.

All things come through desire, and every sincere prayer is answered. We become like that on which our hearts are fixed.

THE UNIVERSE WITHIN

WHEN you ridicule certain traits in others, you ridicule yourself. How would you know that others were contemptible if you did not look into your heart and see the same hateful things?

Thackeray wrote his book on snobs, because he himself was a snob, but not all of the time. When you recognize a thing, good or bad, in the outside world,

> **Atlas could never have carried the world had he fixed his thought on the size of it.**

it is because it is yours already. "I carry the world in my heart," said the prophet of old.

All the universe you have is the universe you have within. Walt Whitman, when he saw a wounded soldier, exclaimed, "I am that man!" and two thousand years before this, Terence said: "I am a man, and nothing that is human is alien to me."

THE CULTURED MIND

CULTIVATE the intellect, and you shall have a mind that produces beautiful thoughts, worthy images, helpful ideas; that will serve as a solace in times of stress, and be to you a refuge against all the storms that blow.

The cultured mind, as compared with the uncultured, is the difference between a beautiful garden which produces vegetables, fruits, and flowers, and a tract of land that is overgrown with weeds and brambles.

To be a person of culture is to be at home under all conditions. Your mind is stored with mental images to guide you from the sense of separateness to universality or oneness with the Divine.

The country will be beautiful to you in any season, and society and solitude will be welcomed by you in turn. You are to reject nothing, despise nothing, knowing that everything belongs some-where, and that it is needed to make up the great mosaic of life.

MEDITATION

To cultivate concentration, practice relaxation. Lie down on the floor for three minutes on your back, breathe deeply, lie still, turn your mind inward, and think of nothing.

To concentrate on your work, you must enjoy your work. And to enjoy your work, you must drop it at certain hours. They last longest, and soar highest, who cultivate the habit of being like children for an hour a day.

Take a vacation every day, if you want to do good work.

TIME

NATURE knows nothing of time—time is for people. And the fleeting quality of time is what makes it so valuable. If life were without limit, we would do nothing. Life without death would be appalling. It would be a day without end—a day with no night of rest.

Death is a change—and death is a manifestation of life. We work because life is short, and through this work we evolve.

VII.

EXERCISE

THE HEALTH HABIT

PEOPLE who live rightly are well; and it is for the doctor to show us how to keep well, and this he will do when he thrives through health and not through our disabilities.

As it is now, we depend on the doctors to cure us if we are sick, and if worst comes to worst, we are fully prepared to go to the hospital and have the surgeon remove the inflamed organ. Wouldn't it be better to so live that no inflammation would follow?

Health is within our reach—it costs nothing, only the effort which soon grows into a pleasurable habit.

Why not acquire the Health Habit? Here is the formula:

First, deep breathing in the open air with your mouth closed.

Second, moderation in eating—simple dishes.

Third, exercise at least an hour in the open each day, walking, working in the garden, playing with the children.

Fourth, sleep eight hours in a thoroughly ventilated room.

Fifth, don't bother to forgive your enemies—just forget them.

Sixth, keep busy—it is a beautiful world, and we can and must leave it more beautiful than we found it.

THE WISDOM OF SYMPTOMS

MY father has practiced medicine for seventy years, and is still practicing. I, also, have studied the so-called science of medicine. I am fifty-five years old; my father is ninety.

We live neighbors, and daily ride horse-back together or tramp through the fields and woods. Today we did our little jaunt of five miles and back across country.

I have never been ill a day—never consulted a physician in a professional way; and, in fact, never missed a meal except through inability of access.

The old gentleman and I are not fully agreed on all of life's themes, so conversation for us never resolves itself into a dull neutral gray. He is a Baptist and I am a vegetarian.

Occasionally he refers to me as "callow," and we have daily resorts to logic to prove prejudice, and history is searched to bolster the preconceived, but on the following important points we stand together, solid as one man:

First—Ninety-nine people out of a hundred who go to a physician have no organic disease, but are merely suffering from some functional disorder caused by their own indiscretion.

Second—Individuals who have organic diseases nine times out of ten are suffering from the accumulated evil effects of medication.

Third—That is to say, most diseases are the result of medication that has been prescribed to relieve and take away a beneficent warning symptom on the part of Nature.

Most of the work of doctors in the past has been to prescribe for symptoms, the difference between actual disease and a symptom being something that the average person does not even yet know.

HAPPINESS & HEALTH

IF you have health, you probably will be happy; and if you have health and happiness, you will have all the wealth you need.

Health is the most natural thing in the world. It is natural to be healthy, because we are a part of Nature—we are Nature. Nature is trying hard to keep us well, because she needs us in her business. Nature needs us so we will be useful to others.

The rewards of life are for service. And the penalties of life are for selfishness.

Human service is the highest form of self-interest for the person who serves. We preserve our sanity only as we forget ourselves in service.

To center on one's self, and forget one's relationship to society, is to summon misery, and misery means disease.

Unhappiness is an irritant. It affects the heart-beats of circulation first; then the digestion; and the person is ripe for two hundred nineteen diseases, and six hundred forty-two complications.

What we call diseases are merely symptoms of metal conditions.

Our bodies are automatic, and thinking about our digestion does not aid us. Rather, it hinders. If we are worried enough, digestion will stop absolutely.

The moral is obvious: Don't Worry.

> **Health and happiness can be found only out of doors.**

AGE & ACTIVITY

IT is a pretty good general rule that, barring accident, you will live as long as you expect to, or, if you please, as long as you want to.

Many people are obsessed with the fallacy that the age of humanity is fixed at the limit of threescore and ten; and so, the vast number of people, when they are around sixty-five, begin to prepare to shuffle off. They quit business, retire from active work, close up their affairs, and when they do these things, death and dissolution are at the door.

Great numbers of very strong, active, earnest people reach the age of eighty, and die at eighty-two, eighty-three, eighty-four. And the reason for this passing is not so much a physical one as it is a mental. They have fixed this age limit in their minds, and their entire life and death conform to the idea.

As a general proposition, I would say the way to live to be one hundred is not to consider the question of time, but simply to continue an active, earnest interest in human affairs, and not over-eat. The individual who looks for ease, rest, and bodily gratification, be he young or old, is in a dangerous position. To eliminate the toxins which accrue in the human body, activity is positively necessary.

The activity of the mind reacts on the organs of the body. So thought is a physical process, and to gain this elimination which insures health, no one should ever think of retiring from business and quitting the game.

Change of occupation is a great factor in human health. If you retire from one thing you must take up something else that is more difficult. Make an earnest vow to "never say die!"

THE FOUNTAIN OF YOUTH

ONE of the things we have recently discovered or rediscovered is that getting old is simply a bad habit.

Those who think they are old, are. And the individual who retires from business will shortly be retired by life. Nature has no use for the person who quits, so she just takes their word for it.

And another curious thing is, that the fear of death is the monopoly of young people. The person who has lived, lives long; and who has kept right at their work, living one day at a time, doing each task the best they could, keeping an interest in all good things—that person is not afraid to die.

Mental work of a congenial kind is a great stimulus to bodily vigor—to think good thoughts, work them out like nuggets of gold, and then coin them into words, is a splendid joy.

And joy is life.

Brain work is just as necessary as physical exercise, and those who play one kind of work off against another find a continual joy and zest in life. The Greeks came near finding this just balance of things; Solon, Sophocles, Pindar, Anacreon, and Xenophon lived to be over eighty, doing strong and excellent work to the last.

Michelangelo was writing love sonnets at eighty-nine, and Titian came within one year of making the century run, and his prayer at the last was that he might live to finish a certain fresco.

I remember seeing Oliver Wendell Holmes when he was eighty-three at Emerson College of Oratory, where, of course, he was dearly beloved by everybody. On the occasion I have in mind, he made a little speech and explained that he was just getting his affairs into shape, that he might come and join the school as a student.

The man's enjoyment in life was complete. He was satisfied, grateful for the past, and filling the present with good work.

Nature's Medicine

THE people you see waiting in the lobbies of doctors' offices are, in a vast majority of cases, suffering through poisoning caused by an excess of food.

Coupled with this goes the bad results of imperfect breathing, irregular sleep, lack of exercise, and improper use of stimulants, or thoughts of fear, jealousy, and hate.

All these things, or any one of them, will, in very many persons, cause fever, chills, cold feet, congestion, and faulty elimination.

To administer drugs to those suffering from malnutrition caused by a desire to "get even," and a lack of fresh air, is simply to compound their troubles, shuffle their maladies, and get them ripe for the ether cone and the scalpel.

Nature is forever trying to keep people well, and most so-called "disease" (which word means merely lack of ease) is self-limiting, and tends to cure itself.

If you have appetite, do not eat too much. If you have no appetite, do not eat at all. Be moderate in the use of all things, save fresh air and sunshine.

The one theme of Ecclesiastes is moderation. Buddha wrote it down that the greatest word in any language is "equanimity." William Morris said that the finest blessing of life was systematic, useful work. Saint Paul declared that the greatest thing in life was love.

Moderation, equanimity, work and love—you need no other physician.

Horseback Riding

I RIDE horseback because I prize my sleep, my digestion, and my mind. That is to say, I ride in order that I may work.

I wish to be a good transformer of divine energy. I want to add to the wealth and happiness of the world, and to make two grins grow where there was only a grouch before. To take care of myself, and then produce a surplus for the benefit of the world, is my ambition.

"We are strong," says Emerson, "only as we ally ourselves with Nature."

I find that when I go in partnership with a good horse, I keep my nerves from getting outside of my clothes. I am better able to act sanely, serenely, and happily, dispose of difficulties and surmount obstacles.

> **Abolish fear and you can accomplish whatever you wish.**

A horse helps you to "forget it." A horse has no troubles of her own. She does not pour into your ear a sad tale of woe.

No one can have melancholia who loves a horse and is understood by one. You shake off your troubles and send your cares flying into the winds when you ride horseback.

I have ridden horseback almost daily for the last forty years. And I enjoy horseback riding today more than ever before.

The individual who keeps his strength and good cheer in this country will never be out of a job. And of work I have always had a plenty.

"I know what pleasure is, for I have done good work," said Robert Louis Stevenson, the well-beloved.

One of the principal reasons why I have been able to do good work is because I have always kept on close, chummy terms with at least one good horse.

Alfred Russel Wallace says that civilization had its rise in the domestication of animals; that where people domesticated the horse, the ox, the camel, the elephant, civilization thrived and they evolved; but that in countries where people had nothing in the way of domestic animals, except a tame wolf—that is, the dog—there was no evolution.

My opinion is that if we are going to preserve our vigor, our courage, our enjoyment, we will have to be on good terms with Mother Earth and close up to *Equus Caballus*.

HEALTH & FEAR

NATURE intended that each species should live to an age approximating five times the number of years that it takes to reach its bodily maturity. Humans reach their maximum height and strength at twenty, and should therefore live to be a hundred.

The brain, being the last organ developed, should sit secure and watch every other organ decline. As it is, the brain, in many individuals who live past seventy, loses its power before the hands and feet, and death reaps something less than a person.

If the sum of human happiness can be increased, life will be much extended.

Of all the mental and physical polluters of life, nothing exercises such a poisonous effect as fear. Fear paralyzes the will, and either stagnates the secretions or turns them loose in a torrent.

Jealousy, cruelty, hate, revenge, all are forms of fear. A person, like a horse, is safe until he gets in the fell clutch of fear. The criminal and the untruthful person are obsessed by fear until the genial current of their life is turned awry.

Abolish fear, and every man and woman is an orator and an artist.

DOCTRINE & DISEASE

MUCH of our sickness is caused by fear, and fear is imported by our beliefs. Our very existence turns on being happy. Misery affects the circulation, fear means congestion, congestion continued means disease, and disease continued means *rigor mortis.*

Now if you were asked what factor in human life had contributed most to fear, would you not be compelled in truth to say, Theology?

Left alone and uninstructed, no one would ever imagine they were "conceived in sin and born in iniquity." Neither would anyone say that we are "born to trouble as the sparks fly upward," or that sickness was sent from God.

Luther died at sixty-three, Calvin at fifty-three, and John Knox at fifty-seven. Luther and Knox were in prison, and Calvin escaped only by flight. All were under sentence of death; all lived under the ban of fear. They were literally scared to death, and their doctrines have since scared to death thousands upon thousands of other people.

Fanaticism is a disease of the mind, just as alcoholism is a disease of the body.

Theology, by diverting our attention from this life to another, and by endeavoring to coerce all people into one religion, constantly preaching that this world is full of misery but the next world will beautiful—or not, as the case may be—has forced on us the thought of fear where otherwise there might have been the happy abandon of nature. Should we not understand the Laws of Life sufficiently, so as to be as well and as happy as birds and squirrels?

The fear of death, as taught by the clergy; the fear of disease, as fostered by the doctors; and the fear of the law, as disseminated by lawyers, has created a fog of fear that has permeated us like a miasma and cut human life short by one-third.

"What, then," you ask; "shall we go back to savagery?"

And my answer is, no—we must, and will, go on to Enlightenment.

VIII.

EXPRESSION

ART & UNDERSTANDING

THE intent of all art is to communicate your feelings and emotions to another. Art has its rise in the need of human companionship.

You feel certain thoughts and you strive to express them. You may express by music, by chiseled shapes, by painted canvas, or by written words. At the last all art is one. And as you work, over against you sits another who says "Yes, yes, I understand!"

The person I write for is a woman. At times she sits nearby and looks at me, leaning forward, resting her chin on her hand. She smiles indulgently, and sometimes a little sadly, as my pen runs on. She knows me so perfectly that she often anticipates what I would say and thus saves me the trouble of writing. She guesses my every mood.

This woman has suffered and known and felt, and that is why she understands. Her heart has been purified in the white fires of experience. She knows more than I, for she sees all around me, and any little effort to palm off a white lie, or the smallest attempt at insincerity or affectation, brings only a wondering look that stings me for a week and a day. I can say anything to her I choose: no topic is forbidden—she asks only that I be honest and frank.

I always know when I have pleased this woman with the wistful eyes, for then she holds out her arms in a slow, sweeping gesture. She is the sister of my soul, and for her I write—because she understands.

SEX & BEAUTY

ONE of nature's chief intents in sex is to bring about beauty, grace, and harmony. It is sex that gives the bird his song, the peacock his gorgeous plumage, the lion his mane, the buffalo his strength, and the horse his proud arch of neck and flowing tail. Aye, it is sex that causes the flowers to draw from the dull earth those delicate perfumes which delight the sense of smell; it is sex, and sex alone, that secures to them the dazzling galaxy of shapes and colors that reflect the Infinite.

All art is a secondary sex manifestation.

The painter knows naught of color, and never could, save as the flowers lead the way. Nature is at once the inspiration and the hopeless tantalization of the artist.

Literature is a matter of passion. Any one who writes well is a lover.

It is love that writes all true poems, paints all pictures, sings all songs.

ARTISTIC CONSCIENCE

WORK to please yourself and you develop and strengthen the artistic conscience. Cling to that and it shall be your mentor in times of doubt; you need no other. There are writers who would scorn to write a muddy line, and would hate themselves for a year and a day should they dilute their thought with the platitudes of fear-ridden people.

> We are moved only by the souls who have suffered and the hearts that know; and so all art that endures is a living, quivering cross-section of life.

Be yourself and speak your mind today, though it contradict all you have said before. And above all, in art work to please yourself—that other self which stands over and behind you, looking over your shoulder, watching your every act, word and deed—knowing your every thought.

Michelangelo would not paint a picture to order.

"I have a critic who is more exacting than you," said Meissonier. "It is my other self."

Rosa Bonheur painted pictures just to please her other self, and never gave a thought to any one else; and having painted to please herself, she made her appeal to the great common heart of humanity—the tender, the noble, the receptive, the earnest, the sympathetic, the lovable. That is why Rosa Bonheur stands first among the women artists of all time; she worked to please her other self.

That is the reason Rembrandt, who lived at the time Shakespeare lived, is today without a rival in portraiture. When at work he never thought of any one but his other self, and so he infused soul into every canvas. The limpid eyes look down into yours from the walls and tell of love, pity, earnestness, and deep sincerity. Humankind, like Deity, creates in its own image. When we portray someone else, we picture ourselves, too—provided our work is art.

If it is but an imitation of something seen somewhere, or done by some one else, or done to please a patron with money, no breath of life has been breathed into its nostrils, and it is nothing, save possibly dead perfection—no more.

It is easy to please your other self? Try it for a day. Begin tomorrow morning and say: "This day I will live as becomes my best self. I will be filled with good-cheer and courage. I will do what is right; I will work for the highest; I will put soul into every hand-grasp, every smile, every expression—my work. I will live to satisfy my other self."

You think it is easy? Try it for a day.

THE POWER OF WORDS

WORDS are tools for the transmission of thoughts. Thoughts are the result of feelings. The recipe for good writing, then, is *write as you feel*—but be sure you feel right.

Before you write you must have a literary kit of expressive, far-reaching words and phrases.

Sidney Smith said that the person who invented a new dish added to the happiness of the world. Whether this is true or not, those who invent a new words give wings to imagination. They link the world together by allowing us to break through the icy silences that surround us.

Through language we touch fingertips with the noble, the great, the good, the competent, living or dead, and thus are we made brothers to all those who make up the sum-total of civilization.

LITERATURE & LIGHT

LIGHT stands for literature. The words have a common root. Literature tokens intelligence, and intelligence mirrors enterprise, thrift, industry. The light seems to give courage, hope, animation, and binds people together into a common bond.

THE GREAT WRITER

THAT writer is great who feeds other minds. He or she inspires others to think for themselves.

That writer is great who tells you the things you already know, but which you did not know you knew until they told you.

That writer is great whom you alternately love and hate. She shocks you, irritates you, affronts you, so that you are jostled out of your wonted ways, pulled out of your mental ruts, lifted out of the mire of the commonplace.

That writer is great whom you cannot forget.

POETRY

THE business of Robert Burns was love-making. Through Burns' penchant for falling in love, we have his songs. Burns' bibliography is simply a record of his love affairs; with the pleas of repentance that followed his lapses made manifest in religious verse.

Poetry is the very earliest form of literature, and is the natural expression of a person in love. Without love there would be no poetry.

All poets are lovers, either actual or potential, and all lovers are poets. Potential poets are the people who read poetry; and so without lovers poets would never have a market for their wares.

If you have ceased to be moved by religious emotion; if your spirit is no longer surged by music; if you do not linger over certain lines of poetry, it is because the love instinct in your heart has withered to ashes of roses.

A VOICE THAT INSPIRES

THE voice is the index of the soul. Children do not pay much attention to your words—they judge your intent by your voice.

We are won or repelled by a voice. If your voice does not corroborate your words, doubt will follow.

Your dog does not obey your words—she does, however, read your intent in your voice.

It is well to cultivate a mild, gentle, and sympathetic voice; and the one way to secure a mild, gentle and sympathetic voice is to be mild, gentle and sympathetic.

If the voice is allowed to come naturally, easily and gently, it will take on every tint and emotion of the mind. If your soul is filled with truth, your voice will vibrate with love, echo with sympathy, and fill your hearers with the desire to do, to be, and to become.

By their voices ye shall know them.

> **Inspiration comes from solitude, a waiting, a communion with the best in us, which is at one with the divine spark.**

ART & ADVERTISING

IT is not deeds or acts that last—it is the written record of those deeds and acts.

The only names in Greek History that we know are those which Herodotus and Thucydides engraved with deathless styli. The reputation that endures, or the institution that lasts, is the one that is properly advertised.

All literature is advertising. And all genuine advertisements are literature.

The author advertises people, places, times, deeds, events and things. You must appeal to the universal human soul. If you do not know the hearts of men and women, their hopes, joys, ambitions, tastes, needs, and desires, your work will interest no one but yourself.

Advertising is fast becoming a fine art. Its theme is Human Wants, and where, when, and how they may be gratified. It interests, inspires, educates, amuses, informs, and thereby uplifts and benefits existence.

Advertising is stating who you are, where you are, and what you have to offer the world in the way of commodity or service. And the only person who should not advertise is the one who has nothing good to offer.

ART & ECONOMY

GOD operates through humanity, and our business is to be a good conductor of the energy we call Life.

Civilization is the efficient way of doing things.

Art is the beautiful way of doing things.

Economy is the cheapest way of doing things.

In order to do things rightly, we must combine efficiency, industry, art, and economy, and cement all with love. Modern commerce must aim at making life pleasant, safe, agreeable, and beautiful.

"Be Yourself" plaque next to a lamp made by
Roycroft master craftsman Dard Hunter

IX.

INDIVIDUALITY

SOME MOCKED, SOME BELIEVED

THE other day I read in a printed book these words, "Some mocked, some shook their heads, and some believed." And that is the universal experience of everyone who ever thought anything or did anything, or was anything. People always mock the thing they are not used to. Afterwards their hilarious mockery may reduce itself to a dubious shaking of the head and a cynical smile; then the smile may fade away into blankness, and they may believe.

Deborah Read, standing in the doorway of her father's house and making fun of the moon-faced Benjamin as he walked up the street munching at his loaves, is typical. Deborah had no flitting ghost of a thought that, one day, this loaf-munching, mirth-moving youth would marry her and give her immortality by linking her name with his—Franklin. No, of course she hadn't.

Saul of Tarsus, going down to Damascus to persecute the Christians, could not foresee that he would come back and henceforth be the foremost Christian of all time.

Some mocked, some shook their heads and some believed.

Yes, be you preacher, lawyer, physician, artist, writer, do your work the best you can and try to live up to your highest ideal, and some will surely mock. If you have genius, a great many will mock, and a great many will shake their heads. But although a great multitude may mock, so long as a few believe, all is well. No good life was ever lived but there was some one believed in it. These few people who believe in us make life possible. Without them, what should we do? But with them we are knitted to the Infinite.

Let the mob mock, let the crowd shake their heads! There are a few who believe.

I know a cottage whose door for me always stands ajar, and where the dwellers therein start with gladness when they hear the coming of my footsteps.

MAKE ROOM FOR INDIVIDUALITY

IT is easier to accept than to investigate. It is easier to be taught than to attain. It is easier to follow than to lead.

Yet we are all heirs to peculiar, unique, and individual talents, and a few of us are not content to follow. These have usually been killed.

> **Conformists die, but heretics live on forever.**

Now our cry is, "Make room for individuality!"

SUPPRESSING GENIUS

FOR teaching the truths of natural science, Giordano Bruno was burned alive in the year 1600, his ashes scattered to the four winds.

Galileo, writing in 1610, complained because the theologians would not so much as look through his telescope, but sat back and declared him an "infidel" and an "atheist."

Two popes, Alexander the Seventh and Urban the Eighth, placed interdicts upon Galileo and forbade his teaching that the earth revolved around the sun, under serious penalty. The works of Galileo and Copernicus were forbidden to all good Catholics for more than two hundred fifty years, placed upon the *Index Librorum Prohibitorum* until 1836.

When you read history, you note the fact that in days gone by nations have killed, banished or disgraced their individuals of genius. This has always been done with the avowed purpose of protecting the state or the prevailing religious system. Socrates, Pericles, Jesus, Anaxagoras, Aristotle, Savonarola, Copernicus, Galileo, Bruno, Huss, Wycliff, are the types that society has suppressed.

Said Bishop John Ireland: "The enemies of the Church have been inside the Church, not outside of it. The supreme blunders of churchmen have been in suppressing strong men—in thwarting individuality. All the good law and all the good order which the State or the Church enjoys today may be traced back over some route to the words and deeds of those who rebelled against the kind of law and the kind of order that they found administered by its constituted guardians; by those who dared to appeal from the 'keepers of divine truth' to divine truth itself—from the 'trustees of God' to God Himself."

INDIVIDUAL FREEDOM

IT is absurd to say we must all live the same way. Yet, whether humanity will ever grow to the point where we are willing to leave life-expression to the individual is a question.

Most people are anxious to do what is best for themselves and least harmful to others. Utopia is not far off, if the folk who govern us, for a consideration, would only be willing to do unto others as they would be done by. War among nations, and strife among individuals, is a result of the covetous spirit to possess power or things.

A little more patience, a little more charity for all, a little more devotion, a little more love, with less bowing down to the past, a brave looking-forward to the future, with more confidence in ourselves and more faith in our fellows, and civilization will be ripe for a great burst of light and life.

THE TYRANNY OF FASHION

ONCE, in my callow days, I accepted a wager that I could wear a prison suit and walk from Buffalo to Cleveland without serious molestation.

It took me over four days to get thirty miles. I was arrested nine times, and at Dunkirk I came near being mobbed by Sunday School picnickers, and was compelled to give up my uniform for citizens clothes. Yet I was a free man and innocent of crime, and there was no law defining what I should wear.

But there are unwritten laws, and to a great degree society dictates what its members shall wear; as in feudal times, and much the same today, the master dictates to his servants what their clothing shall be.

> Do nothing, say nothing, be nothing, and you'll never be criticized.

And the master himself is caught in the mesh that he has woven, and this soulless something we call Society dictates to him what he shall do and what not. There are limits beyond which he can not go. So those who make fashions are caught and held captive by them, just as the children who play ghost get badly frightened themselves.

LIVE YOUR OWN LIFE

IF you are defamed, let time vindicate you—silence is a thousand times better than explanation. Explanations do not explain.

All wrong recoils upon the doer, and the individual who makes wrong statements about others is to be pitied, not the one he vilifies. It is better to be lied about than to lie.

Let your life be its own excuse for being—cease all explanations and all apologies, and just live your life. In the end, no one can harm us but ourselves.

By minding your own business you give others an opportunity to mind theirs; and depend upon it, the great souls will appreciate you for this very thing.

I am not sure that absolute, perfect justice comes to everyone in this world, but I do know that the best way to get justice is not to be too anxious about it.

As love goes to those who do not lie in wait for it, so do the great rewards gravitate to the patient.

> Never explain—your friends do not need it, and your enemies will not believe you anyway.

The Courage to Change

THERE is no doubt that a teacher once committed to a certain line of thought will cling to that line long after all others have deserted it. In trying to convince others, they convince themselves.

Thus we see why institutions are so conservative. Like the coral insect, they secrete osseous matter; and when a preacher preaches, he himself goes forward to the altar and accepts all the dogmas that have just been so ably stated.

Faith in your own opinions is a good thing, but—were you ever absolutely certain of the result of an election, prophesying a total wave for "our party"—and the next morning awake to find that the basis for your belief was built on the East Wind?

Did you ever go to a horse-race and lay your money on a Sure Thing and never see the hard-earned again?

Have you ever fought valiantly for a creed, or a platform, and then in a few years, conclude, of your own accord, that you were on the wrong track, and turn around and denounce the thing you once upheld?

Well, if so, and you have thus learned to dilute faith in your own infallibility with a little doubt, you have not lived in vain.

X.

INTERDEPENDENCE

A Declaration of Interdependence

I HOLD these truths to be self-evident:
That people were made to be happy;

That happiness is only attainable through useful effort;

That the best way to help ourselves is to help others;

That useful effort means the proper exercise of all our faculties;

That we grow, only through this exercise;

That education should continue through life;

That where people alternate work, study, and play in right proportion, the brain is the last organ of the body to fail, and death for such people has no terrors;

That the possession of wealth can never make a person exempt from useful, manual labor;

That if all would work a little, none would be overworked;

That if no one wasted, all would have enough;

That if none were overfed, none would be underfed;

That the rich and "educated" need education quite as much as the poor and illiterate;

That the presence of a serving class is an indictment and a disgrace to our civilization;

That the disadvantage of having a serving class falls most upon those who are served, and not upon those who serve—just as the curse of slavery falls upon the slave-owner;

That the people who are waited on by a serving class cannot have a just consideration for the rights of others;

That those who live on the labor of others, not giving themselves in return to the best of their ability, are really consumers of human life;

That the best way to abolish a serving class is for all to join it;

That in useful service there is no high nor low;

That all duties, offices, and things useful and necessary are sacred.

STRENGTH IN OTHERS

A BEE alone can make no honey. A bee alone is not self-supporting. In fact, separated a distance of from three to five miles from its hive, it will soon droop and die. Bees are successful only as they work with other bees.

A person alone will accomplish nothing. All of your thoughts and acts have a direct relationship with others. Individuals succeed only as they work together. Without companionship, ambition droops; courage flags; reason totters; animation vanishes, and the individual dies.

Soldiers who are cowards when by themselves often fight bravely when placed on the firing line with others.

Do not separate yourself from plain people; be one with all— be universal.

We succeed only as we band ourselves together with others. A superintendent of the Pennsylvania Railroad tells me that he has found that four men working together will do at least five times as much work as one man working alone, and they will also do the work better. Teachers know the principle, and thus they teach in classes. Children will teach each other quite as much as they are taught by their teachers.

Healthy people like to work, play, eat, learn, and live together. The Kindergarten Spirit (and no finer thing exists) is possible only through association.

A child absolutely alone would never evolve. A child deprived of the companionship of its own becomes abnormal. Great is the one who carries the Kindergarten Spirit right through life.

FRIENDSHIP

T HE desire for friendship is strong in every human heart. We crave the companionship of those who understand. The nostalgia of life presses, we sigh for "home," and long for the presence of one who sympathizes with our aspirations, comprehends our hopes, and is able to partake of our joys. A thought is not our own until we impart it to another, and the confessional seems to be a crying need of every human soul.

One can bear grief, but it takes two to be glad. We reach the divine through some one, and by dividing our joy with this one we double it, and come in touch with the Universal. The sky is never so blue, the birds never sing so blithely, our acquaintances are never so gracious, as when we are filled with love for some one else.

Being in harmony with one we are in harmony with all.

CONSIDER THE BEE

IT has been said, "Humanity is the most wonderful of all the works of God"—but no one ever said so but a human.

Bees can do things we cannot, and they know things a human never will.

A queen bee will lay over a million eggs during the summer. The eggs she lays every day are about double her own weight. These eggs are all alike when they hatch, but by feeding the larva differently, bees produce drones, workers, or queens, at will.

It only takes three days for the eggs to hatch. The young are then fed by the nurse bees, which are the bees under sixteen days old. These nurse bees feed the others from glands in their heads that secrete milk.

When the bee is sixteen days old she is of age and goes to work. The average life of the worker is only forty-five days. She just works herself to death, unless winter comes on and then she may live through until the next year.

There are about fifty thousand bees in a hive; thirty-five thousand workers and fifteen thousand nurse bees or housekeepers. Then there are six hun-

We help ourselves only as we help others, and the love we give away is the only love we keep.

dred drones and one queen. The queen often lives for five years, but the drones never live over winter. As soon as the first sign of winter comes and the flowers begin to wither, the bees have a St. Bartholomew's day and kill every drone. Drones have no stingers, but queens and workers have. The workers are females—undeveloped queens.

Bees have five eyes, three they use for seeing in the dark and for reading, and two for long-distance hustling.

When a hive gets too full, the bees swarm, the old ones going away led by the queen. As soon as the old queen goes, the bees that remain at home immediately grow a new queen.

Bees are very orderly and cleanly. They have inspectors that stay at the door of the hive and see that no bee comes in from the field without a good load of honey. Often if the bee has only a little honey, the inspector will turn her back and give her what is coming to her.

Bees very seldom die in the hive: if they do, it is a sign the whole hive is weak. The bees clean out all dust and dirt with great care, and if a bug or mouse gets into the hive they will straightway kill the intruder. Then, if the body is too big for them to drag out, they will cover it over and seal it up with propolis, a sticky substance that bees gather from buds or the bark of trees.

A hive of thirty-five thousand workers will often bring in twenty pounds of honey in a day, if the flowers are just right; and one man I know who owns eighty-five hives, has had his bees make a ton of honey in ten hours. And yet one bee only gathers a grain of honey a day, and may visit three hundred flowers to get it.

The wax is a secretion from the bee's body, but the honey they get from the flowers. The object of the honey in the flower is that the insect will come and get itself dusted with pollen, which they carry to other flowers. So besides gathering honey, bees do a very necessary work in the fertilization of flowers. In fact, you cannot raise white clover without bees, and bees do not thrive at their best excepting when they find white clover, so thus does nature understand her business.

> **Better mend one fault in yourself than a hundred in your neighbor.**

Occasionally a bee will go off to the fields and come back gorged with honey, bringing nothing for the common stock, and this bee is quickly killed—stung to death by a self-appointed committee who sit on the case, and seem to consider that any bee which loses sight of the Spirit of the Hive and works for private good is sick, criminally insane, and cannot be allowed longer to cumber good space.

With the bee, there is seemingly no evolution. The Spirit of the Hive is fixed within narrow limits. With human beings, the Spirit of the Hive—or, if you prefer, the Spirit of the Times, or the *Zeitgeist*—is a constantly changing spiritual entity.

Everyone who expresses what he or she honestly think is true is changing the Spirit of the Times. Those who write their thoughts help other people to think. No person writes or thinks alone—thought is in the air, but its expression is necessary to create a tangible Spirit of the Times.

THE SPIRIT OF THE HIVE

B EES succeed only by working for the good of other bees. A single bee, separated from the hive, is absolutely helpless, yet a hive of bees has a very great and well-defined purpose and intelligence. This intelligence, Maeterlinck calls the "Spirit of the Hive."

THE GENIUS OF GROUPS

G ENIUS has always come in groups, because groups produce the friction that generates light.

Competition with fools is not bad—fools teach the imbecility of repeating their performances. You learn to cut out absurdity, strengthen here and bolster there, until in your soul there grows up an ideal, which you may materialize in stone or bronze, on canvas, or by spoken word.

Greece had her group when the wit of Aristophanes sought to overtop the stately lines of Aeschylus; Praxiteles outdid Ictinus; while the words of Socrates outlasted them all.

Rome had her group when all the arts sought the silver speech of Cicero.

One artist never flourishes alone—they go together, each doing the thing they can do best. All the arts are really one, and this one art is simply expression—the expression of Mind speaking through its highest instrument, humanity.

> **As we grow better, we meet better people.**

THE COMMUNITY OF TRUTH-SEEKERS

I LONG to be a citizen of the Eternal City of Fine Minds. I would belong to that brother-and-sisterhood which cultivates the receptive heart and the generous mind. My neighbors are often hundreds of miles apart. They are the men and women of earth who think and feel and dream, who ask themselves each morning, "What is Truth?"

That is the question Pilate asked, and we think better of him for it. But Jesus did not answer. He could not. All truth is relative, and the message which comes to you from out of the great Silence can only be interpreted to another who has listened and heard.

RESOLVED. THAT WE DON'T LIKE MEN WHO BUTTON THEIR COLLARS
BEHIND AND HAVE SUNDAY SCHOOL IN-DOORS, WHERE DOGS ARE NOT WELCOME;
    THAT WE LIKE THE FRA, BECAUSE HE LOVES KIDDIES, KIDDEENS AND
KIOODLES, AND STANDS FOR HEALTH AND HAPPINESS AND AGREES WITH
TIGE THAT VIVISECTION IS WORSE THAN HYDROPHOBIA BECAUSE A DOG
THAT BITES A MAN CANT HELP IT, BUT A MAN WHO STRAPS A DOG ON A TABLE. &
CUTS INTO HIM WITH A KNIFE AND SCISSORS NEEDN'T IF HE DOESN'T WANT
TO;
        THAT BOYS AND GIRLS DO NOT LIKE THE STUFFY IN-DOORS;
THAT TO GET ACQUAINTED WITH BEES, BUGS, BIRDS AND BEETLES IS
LOTS MORE FUN AND JUST AS MUCH BENEFIT AS READING ABOUT NICODEMUS
& NEBUCHADNEZZAR WHO ARE DEAD ONES, BOTH; THAT BAD CHILDREN
ARE GOOD CHILDREN WHO HAVE ENERGY PLUS, AND THEIR PARENTS SAY,
"QUIT THAT", "LET UP", "GET OUT";
    THAT DIRTY CLOTHES ARE PREFERABLE TO PALE CHEEKS, AND
THAT WE SHOULD ALL LIVE IN HEAVEN HERE AND NOW, SO TO GET
USED TO IT FOR BY AND BY   BUSTER BROWN.

"Fra Elbertus" making an appearance in the nation's most popular
newspaper comic, R. F. Outcault's Buster Brown

THE ROYCROFT IDEA:
A PERSONAL HISTORY

I HAVE been asked to write an article about myself and the work in which I am engaged. Let me begin by telling what I am not, and thus reach the vital issue by elimination.

First, I am not popular in "society," and those who champion my cause in my own town are plain, unpretentious people.

Second, I am not a popular writer, since my name has never been mentioned in the *Atlantic, Scribner's, Harper's, The Century,* or the *Ladies' Home Journal.* In days agone, I waited long hours in the entryway of each of the magazines just named, and then was handed my hat.

Third, I am not rich, as the world counts wealth.

Fourth, as an orator I am without the graces, and do scant justice to the double-breasted Prince Albert.

Fifth, the Roycroft Shop, to the welfare of which my life is dedicated, is not so large as to be conspicuous on account of size.

Sixth, personally, I am no ten-thousand-dollar beauty: the glass of fashion and the mold of form are far from mine.

Then what have I done concerning which the public wishes to know? Simply this:

In one obscure country village I have had something to do with stopping the mad desire on the part of the young people to get out of the country and flock to the cities. In this town and vicinity, the tide has been turned from city to country. We have made one country village an attractive place for growing youth by supplying congenial employment, opportunity for education, healthful recreation, and an outlook into the world of art and beauty.

All boys and girls want to make beautiful things with their hands, and they want to "get along," and I've simply given them a chance to get along here instead of seeking their fortunes in Buffalo, New York, or Chicago. They have helped me and I have helped them; and through this mutual help we have gained ground.

We don't live unto ourselves alone: our interests are all bound up together, and there is no such thing as a person going off alone and corralling the good. By myself I could have done nothing, and if I have succeeded, it is simply because I have had the aid and cooperation of cheerful, willing, loyal, and loving helpers. Even now as I am writing this in my cabin in the woods, four miles from the village, they are down there at the Shop, quietly, patiently, cheerfully doing my work—which work is also theirs.

IN London, from about 1650 to 1690, Samuel and Thomas Roycroft printed and made very beautiful books. In choosing the name "Roycroft" for our Shop we had these men in mind, but beyond this the word has a special significance, meaning King's Craft— King's craftsmen being a term used in the Guilds of the olden times for those who had achieved a high degree of skill— those who made things for the King. So a Roycrofter is a person who makes beautiful things, and makes them as well as he or she can. "The Roycrofters" is the legal name of our institution. It is a corporation, and the shares are distributed among the workers. No shares are held by any one but Roycrofters, and it is agreed that any worker who quits the Shop shall sell his shares back to the concern. This cooperative plan, it has been found, begets a high degree of personal diligence, a loyalty to the institution, a sentiment of fraternity and a feeling of permanency among the workers that is very beneficial to all concerned. Each worker, even the most humble, calls it "Our Shop," and feels that he or she is an integral and necessary part of the Whole. Possibly there are a few who consider themselves more than necessary. And this is all right, too—I would never chide an excess of zeal: the pride of a worker in their worth and work is a thing to foster.

It's the one who "doesn't give a damn" who is really troublesome. The artistic big-head is not half so bad as apathy.

IN December, 1894, I printed the first *Little Journeys* in booklet form, at the local printing-office, having become discouraged in trying to find a publisher. But before offering the publication to the public, I decided to lay the matter again before G. P. Putnam's Sons, although they had declined the matter in manuscript form. Mr. George H. Putnam rather liked the matter, and was induced to issue the periodical as a venture for one year. The scheme seemed to meet with success—subscriptions reached nearly a thousand in six months; the newspapers were kind, and the success of the plan suggested printing a pamphlet modeled on similar lines, telling what we thought about things in general.

There was no intention at first of issuing more than one number of this pamphlet, but to get it through the mails at magazine rates we made up a little subscription list and asked that it be entered at the post office at East Aurora as second-class matter. The postmaster adjusted his brass-rimmed spectacles, read the pamphlet, and decided that it surely was second class matter.

We called it *The Philistine* because we were going after the "chosen people" in literature. It was Leslie Stephen who said, "The term Philistine is a word used by prigs to designate people they do not like." When you call someone a bad name, you are that thing—not them. The smug and snugly ensconced denizens of Union Square called me a Philistine, and I said, "Yes, I am one, if a Philistine is something different from you."

My helpers, the printers, were about to go away to pastures new; they were in debt, the town was small, they could not make a living. So they offered me their outfit for a thousand dollars. I accepted the proposition.

I decided to run *The Philistine* magazine for a year—to keep faith with the misguided and hopeful parties who had subscribed—and then quit. To fill in the time, we printed a book: we printed it like a William Morris book, just as well as we could. It was cold in the old barn where we first set up *The Philistine*, so I built a little building like an old English chapel right alongside of my house. There was one basement and a room upstairs. I wanted it to be comfortable and pretty, and so we furnished our little shop cozily. We had four girls and three boys working for us then. The Shop was never locked, and the boys and girls used to come around evenings. It was really more pleasant than at home.

I brought over a shelf of books from the library. Then I brought the piano, because the youngsters wanted to dance.

The girls brought flowers and birds, and the boys put up curtains at the windows. We were having a lot of fun, with new subscriptions coming in almost every day, and once in a while an order for a book.

The place got too small when we began to bind books, so we built a wing on one side; then a wing on the other

> **It is the finest thing in the world to live—most people only exist.**

side. To keep the three carpenters busy who had been building the wings, I set them to making furniture for the place. They made the furniture as good as they could—folks came along and bought it.

The boys picked up field-stones and built a great, splendid fireplace and chimney at one end of the Shop. The work came out so well that I said, "Boys, here is a great scheme—these hardheads are splendid building material." So I advertised we would pay a dollar a load for large stones. The farmers began to haul stones; they hauled more stones, and at last they had hauled four thousand loads. We bought all the stone in the dollar limit, cornering the market on boulders.

Three stone buildings have been built, another is in progress, and our plans are made to build an art-gallery of the same material—the stones that the builders rejected.

An artist blew in on the way to nowhere, his baggage a tomato-can. He thought he would stop over for a day or two—he is with us yet, and three years have gone by since he came, and now we could not do without him.

We have boys who have been expelled from school, blind people, deaf people, old people, jailbirds and mental defectives, and have managed to set them all at useful work.

We do not encourage people from a distance who want work to come on—they are apt to expect too much. They look for Utopia, when work is work, here as elsewhere. There is just as much need for patience, gentleness, loyalty, and love here as anywhere.

We do our work as well as we can, live one day at a time, and try to be kind.

THE village of East Aurora, Erie County, New York, the home of The Roycrofters, is eighteen miles southeast of the city of Buffalo. The place has a population of about three thousand people.

There is no wealth in the town and no poverty. In East Aurora there are six churches, and we have a most excellent school. The place is not especially picturesque or attractive, being simply a representative New York State village.

Most of the workers in the Roycroft Shop are children of farming folk, and it is needless to add that they are not college-bred, nor have they had the advantages of foreign travel. One of our best helpers, Uncle Billy Bushnell, has never been to Niagara Falls, and does not care to go. Uncle Billy says if you stay at home and do your work well enough, the world will come to you.

The wisdom of this hard-headed old son of the soil—who abandoned agriculture for art at seventy—is exemplified in the fact that during the year just past, over twenty-eight thousand pilgrims have visited the Roycroft Shop—representing every state and territory of the Union and every civilized country on the globe, even far-off Iceland, New Zealand and the Isle of Guam.

Three hundred ten people are on the payroll at the present writing. The principal work is printing, illuminating and binding books. We also have a furniture shop, where Mission furniture of the highest grade is made; a modeled-leather shop, where the most wonderful creations in calfskin are to be seen; and a smithy, where copper utensils of great beauty are hammered out by hand.

Quite as important as the printing and binding is the illuminating of initials and title-pages. This is a revival of a lost art, gone with so much of the artistic work done by the monks of the olden time. Yet there is a demand for such work; and so far as I know, we are the first concern in America to take up the hand-illumination of books as a business. Of course we have had to train our helpers, and from very crude attempts at decoration we have attained to a point where the British Museum and the Bibliotheke at The Hague have deigned to order and pay good golden guineas for specimens of our handicraft. Very naturally we want to do the best work possible, and so self-interest prompts us to be on the lookout for budding genius. The Roycroft is a quest for talent.

> **Our finest flowers are often weeds transplanted.**

There is a market for the best, and the surest way, we think, to get away from competition is to do your work a little better than the other fellow. The tendency to make things cheaper, instead of better, in the book business is a fallacy, as shown in the fact that within ten years there have been a dozen failures of big publishing-houses in the United States. The liabilities of these bankrupt concerns footed the fine total of fourteen million dollars. The one who made more books and cheaper books than any one concern ever made, had the felicity to fail very shortly, with liabilities of something over a million dollars. They overdid the thing in matter of cheapness—mistook their market. Our motto is, "Not how cheap, but how good."

This is the richest country the world has ever known, far richer per capita than England. Once Americans were all shoddy—pioneers have to be, I'm told—but now only a part of us are shoddy. As men and women increase in culture and refinement, they want better things. The cheap article, I will admit, ministers to a certain grade of intellect; but if as people grow, there will come a time when, instead of a great many cheap and shoddy things, they will want a few good things. They will want things that symbolize solidity, truth, genuineness and beauty.

THE Roycrofters have many opportunities for improvement, not the least of which is the seeing, hearing, and meeting distinguished people. We have a public dining-room, and not a day passes but men and women of note sit and sup with us. At the evening meal, if our visitors are so inclined, I ask them to talk. And if there is no one else to speak, I sometimes read a little from William Morris, Shakespeare, Walt Whitman, or Ruskin. David Bispham has sung for us. Maude Adams and Minnie Maddern Fiske have favored us with a taste of their quality. Judge Lindsey, Alfred Henry Lewis, Richard Le Gallienne, and Robert Barr have visited us.

To give a list of all the eminent men and women who have spoken, sung, or played for us would lay me liable for infringement in reprinting *Who's Who*. However, let me name one typical incident. The Boston Ideal Opera Company was playing in Buffalo, and Henry Clay Barnabee and half a dozen of his players took a run out to East Aurora. They were shown through the Shop by one of the girls whose work it is to receive visitors. A young woman of the company sat down at one of the pianos and played. I chanced to be near and asked Mr. Barnabee if he would sing, and graciously he answered, "Fra Elbertus, I'll do anything that you say." I gave the signal that all the workers should quit their tasks and meet at the Chapel. In five minutes we had an audience of three hundred—men in blouses and overalls, girls in big aprons—a very jolly, kindly, receptive company.

Mr. Barnabee was at his best—I never saw him so funny. He sang, danced, recited, and told stories for forty minutes. The Roycrofters were, of course, delighted.

ONE fortuitous event that has worked to our decided advantage was "A Message to Garcia."

This article, covering only fifteen hundred words, was written one evening after supper in a single hour. It was the twenty-second of February, 1899, Washington's Birthday, and we were just going to press with the March *Philistine*. The thing leaped hot from my heart, written after a rather trying day, when I had been endeavoring to train some rather delinquent helpers in the way they should go.

The immediate suggestion, though, came from a little argument over the teacups when my son Bert suggested that Rowan was the real hero of the Cuban war. Rowan had gone alone and done the thing—carried the message to Garcia.

It came to me like a flash! Yes, the boy is right, the hero is the man who does the thing—does his work—carries the message.

I got up from the table and wrote "A Message to Garcia."

I thought so little of it that we ran it in without a heading. The edition went out, and soon orders began to come for extra March *Philistines*, a dozen, fifty, a hundred; and when the American News Company ordered a thousand I asked one of my helpers which article it was that had stirred things up.

"It's that stuff about Garcia," he said.

The next day a telegram came from George H. Daniels, of the New York Central Railroad, thus: "Give price on one hundred thousand Rowan article in pamphlet form— Empire State Express advertisement on back— also state how soon can ship."

I replied giving price and stated we could supply the pamphlets in two years. Our facilities were small, and a hundred thousand pamphlets looked like an awful undertaking.

The result was that I gave Mr. Daniels permission to reprint the article in his own way. He issued it in booklet form in editions of one hundred thousand each. Five editions were sent out, and then he got out an edition of half a million. Two or three of these half-million lots were sent out by Mr. Daniels, and in addition the article was reprinted in over two hundred magazines and newspapers. It has been translated into eleven languages, and given a total circulation of over twenty-two million copies. It has attained, I believe, a larger circulation in the same length of time than any written article has ever before reached.

Of course, we can not tell just how much good "A Message to Garcia" has done the Shop, but it probably doubled the circulation of *The Philistine*. I do not consider it by any means my best piece of writing; but it was opportune—the time was ripe. Truth demands a certain expression, and too much had been said on the other side about the downtrodden, honest man, looking for work and not being able to find it. The article in question states the other side. Men are needed— loyal, honest men who will do their work. "The world cries out for him—the man who can carry a message to Garcia."

> There are no secrets in life, because Nature has provided that your every thought and sentiment will shine out of your face.

CONCERNING my own personal history, I'll not tarry long to tell. It has been much like the career of many another born in the semi-pioneer times of the Middle West.

I was born in Illinois, June nineteenth, 1856. My father was a country doctor, whose income never exceeded five hundred dollars a year. I left school at fifteen, with a fair hold on the three R's, and beyond this my education in "manual training" had been good. I knew all the forest-trees, all wild animals thereabout, every kind of fish, frog, fowl, or bird. I knew every kind of grain or vegetable and its comparative value. I knew the different breeds of cattle, horses, sheep, and swine.

I could teach wild cows to stand while being milked; break horses to saddle or harness; could sow, plow and reap; knew the mysteries of apple-butter, pumpkin pie, pickled beef, smoked side-meat, and could make lye and formulate soft soap.

That is to say, I was a bright, strong, active country boy who had been brought up to help his father and mother get a living for a large family.

At fifteen I worked on a farm and did a man's work for a boy's pay. I did not like it and told the man so. He replied, "You know what you can do."

And I replied, "Yes." I went westward like the course of empire and became a cowboy; tired of this and went to Chicago; worked in a printing office; peddled soap from house to house; shoved lumber on the docks; read all the books I could find; wrote letters back to country newspapers and became a reporter; next got a job as traveling salesman; taught in a district school; read Emerson, Carlyle, and Macaulay; worked in a soap factory; read Shakespeare and committed most of *Hamlet* to memory with an eye on the stage; became manager of the soap-factory, then partner; evolved an idea for the concern and put it on the track of making millions—knew it was going to make millions—did not want them; sold out my interest for seventy-five thousand dollars and went to Harvard College; tramped through Europe; wrote for sundry newspapers; penned two books (couldn't find a publisher); taught night school in Buffalo; tramped through Europe some more and met William Morris (caught it); came back to East Aurora and started Chautauqua Circles; studied Greek and Latin with a local clergyman; raised trotting-horses; and wrote *Little Journeys to the Homes of Good Men and Great*.

That is how I got my education, such as it is. I am a graduate of the University of Hard Knocks, and I've taken several postgraduate courses. I have worked at five different trades enough to be familiar with the tools. In 1899, Tufts College bestowed on me the degree of

> God always gives us strength to bear the troubles of each day; but He never calculated on our piling troubles past, and yet to come, on top of those of today.

Master of Arts; but since I did not earn the degree, it really does not count.

I have never been sick a day, never lost a meal through disinclination to eat, never consulted a doctor, never used tobacco or intoxicants. My work has never been regulated by the eight-hour clause.

Horses have been my only extravagance, and I ride daily now on a horse that I broke myself, that has never been saddled by another, and that has never been harnessed.

My best friends have been working-men, homely women, and children. My father and mother are members of my household, and they work in the Shop when they are so inclined. My mother's business now is mostly to care for the flowers, and my father we call "Physician to The Roycrofters," as he gives free advice and attendance to all who desire his services. Unfortunately for him, we do not enjoy poor health, so there is very seldom any one sick to be cured. Fresh air is free, and outdoor exercise is not discouraged.

THE Roycroft Shop and belongings represent an investment of about three hundred thousand dollars. We have no liabilities, making it a strict business policy to sign no notes or other instruments of debt that may in the future prove inopportune and tend to disturb digestion. Fortune has favored us.

First, the country has grown tired of soft platitude, silly truism, and undisputed things said in such a solemn way. So when *The Philistine* stepped into the ring and voiced in no uncertain tones what its editor thought, thinking men and women stopped and listened. Editors of magazines refused my writing because they said it was too plain, too blunt, sometimes indelicate—it would give offense, subscribers would cancel, et cetera. To get my thoughts published I had to publish them myself; and people bought for the very reason for which the editors said they would wouldn't.

The editors were wrong. They failed to properly diagnose a demand. The readers wanted brevity and plain statement—I saw the demand and filled it.

Next, I believed in the American public. A portion of it, at least, wanted a few good and beautiful books instead of a great many cheap books. The truth came to me when John B. Alden and half a dozen other publishers of cheap books went to the wall. I read the R. G. Dun & Company bulletin and I said, "The publishers have mistaken their public—we want better books, not cheaper." In 1892, I met William Morris, and after that I was sure I was right.

Again I had gauged the public correctly, while the publishers were wrong.

Next the public wanted to know about this thing—"What are you folks doing out there in that buckwheat town?" Since in my twenties I had one eye on the stage, I could talk in public a bit. I had made political speeches, given entertainments in schoolhouses, made temperance harangues, was always called upon to introduce the speaker of the evening, and several times had given readings from my own amusing works for the modest stipend of ten dollars and keep. I would have taken the lecture platform had it not been nailed down.

In 1898, my friend Major Pond wanted to book me on a partnership deal at the Waldorf-Astoria. I didn't want to speak there—I had been saying unkind things in *The Philistine* about the Waldorf-Astoria folks. But the Major went ahead and made arrangements. I expected to be mobbed.

But Mr. Boldt, the manager of the hotel, treated me most cordially. He never referred to the outrageous things I had said about his tavern; assured me that he enjoyed my writings, and told me of the pleasure he had in welcoming me. The Astor gallery seats eight hundred people. Major Pond had packed in nine hundred at one dollar each—and three hundred were turned away. After the lecture the Major awaited me in the anteroom, and fell on my neck crying: "Oh, why didn't we charge them two dollars apiece!"

The next move was to make a tour of the principal cities under Major Pond's management. Neither of us lost money—the Major surely did not.

Last season I gave eighty-one lectures. I spoke at Tremont Temple in Boston, to twenty-two hundred people; at Carnegie Hall, New York; at Central Music Hall, Chicago. I spoke to all the house would hold; at Chautauqua, my audience was five thousand people. It will be noted by the discerning that my lectures have been of double importance, in that they have given an income and at the same time advertised the Roycroft wares.

THE success of the Roycroft Shop has not been brought about by any one scheme or plan. The business is really a combination of several ideas:

First, the printing and publication of three magazines.

Second, the printing of books (it being well known that some of the largest publishers in America—Scribner and Appleton, for instance—have no printing-plants, but have the work done for them).

Third, the publication of books.

Fourth, the artistic binding of books.

Fifth, authorship. Since I began printing my own manuscripts, there has been an eager demand for my writing.

Sixth, the Lecture Lyceum.

Seventh, blacksmithing, carpenter-work and basket-weaving. These industries have sprung up under the Roycroft care as a necessity. Men and women in the village came to us and wanted work, and we simply gave them opportunity to do the things they could do best. We have found a market for all our wares, so no line of work has ever been a bill of expense.

I want no better clothing, no better food, no more comforts and conveniences than my helpers and fellow-workers have. I would be ashamed to monopolize a luxury—to take a beautiful work of art, say a painting or a marble statue, and keep it for my own pleasure and for the select few I might invite to see my beautiful things. Art is for all— beauty is for all. Harmony in all of its manifold forms should be like a sunset—free to all who can drink it in. The Roycroft Shop is for the Roycrofters, and each is limited only by their capacity to absorb.

> A retentive memory may be a good thing, but the ability to forget is the true token of greatness.

ART is the expression of our joy in our work, and all the joy and love that you can weave into a fabric comes out again and belongs to the individual who has the soul to appreciate it. Art is beauty; and beauty is a gratification, a peace, and a solace to every normal man and woman. Beautiful sounds, beautiful colors, beautiful proportions, beautiful thoughts—how our souls hunger for them! Matter is only mind in an opaque condition; and all beauty is but a symbol of spirit. You cannot get joy from feeding things all day into a machine. You must let a person work with hand and brain, and then out of the joy of this marriage of hand and brain, beauty will be born. It tells of a desire for harmony, peace, beauty, wholeness—holiness.

Art is the expression of joy in our work.

When you read a beautiful poem that makes your heart throb with gladness and gratitude, you are simply partaking of the emotion that the author felt when she wrote it. To possess a piece of work that the artist made in joyous animation is a source of joy to the possessor.

And this love of the work done by the marriage of hand and brain can never quite go out of fashion—for we are men and women, and our hopes and aims and final destiny are at last one. Where one enjoys, all enjoy; where one suffers, all suffer.

Say what you will of the coldness and selfishness of humanity, at the last we long for companionship and the fellowship of our kind. We are lost children, and when alone and the darkness gathers, we long for the close relationship of the brothers and sisters we knew in our childhood, and cry for the gentle arms that once rocked us to sleep. We are homesick amid this sad, mad rush for wealth and place and power. The calm of the country invites, and we would fain do with less things, and go back to simplicity, and rest our tired heads in the lap of Mother Nature.

Life is expression. Life is a movement outward, an unfolding, a development. To be tied down, pinned to a task that is repugnant, and to have the shrill voice of necessity whistling eternally in your ears, "Do this or starve," is to starve; for it starves the heart, the soul, and all the higher aspirations of your being pine away and die.

> **The Mintage of Wisdom is to know that Rest is Rust, and that real life is Love, Laughter, and Work.**

At the Roycroft Shop the workers are getting an education by doing things. Work should be the spontaneous expression of our best impulses. We grow only through exercise, and every faculty that is exercised becomes strong, and those not used atrophy and die. Thus how necessary it is that we should exercise our highest and best!

To develop the brain we have to exercise the body. Every muscle, every organ, has its corresponding convolution in the brain. To develop the mind, we must use the body. Manual training is essentially moral training; and physical work is, at its best, mental, moral, and spiritual—and these are truths so great

and yet so simple that until yesterday many did not recognize them.

At the Roycroft Shop we are reaching out for an all-round development through work and right living.

And we have found it a good expedient—a wise business policy. Sweat-shop methods can never succeed in producing beautiful things. And so the management of the Roycroft Shop surrounds the workers with beauty, allows many liberties, encourages cheerfulness, and tries to promote kind thoughts, simply because it has been found that these things are transmuted into good, and come out again at the finger-tips of the workers in beautiful results.

So we have pictures, statuary, flowers, ferns, palms, birds, and a piano in every room. We have the best sanitary appliances that money can buy; we have bathrooms, shower-baths, library, rest-rooms. Every week we have concerts, dances, lectures.

Besides being a workshop, the Roycroft is a School. We are following out a dozen distinct lines of study, and every worker in the place is enrolled as a member of one or more classes. There are no fees to pupils, but each pupil purchases their own books—the care of one's books and belongings being considered a part of one's education. All the teachers are workers in the Shop, and are volunteers, teaching without pay, beyond what each receives for his regular labor.

The art of teaching, we have found, is a great benefit—to the teacher. The teacher gets most out of the lessons. It is responsibility that develops a person, and to know that your pupils expect you to know is a great incentive to study. Then teaching demands that you shall give—give yourself—and those who give most receive most. We deepen our impressions by recounting them, and those who teach others teach themselves. I am never quite so proud as when some one addresses me as "teacher."

The thing that pays should be the expedient thing, and the expedient thing should be the proper and right thing. That which began with us as a matter of expediency is often referred to as a "philanthropy." I do not like the word, and wish to state here that the Roycroft is in no sense a charity—I do not believe in giving any one something for nothing. You give a person a dollar and he will think less of you because he thinks less of himself; but if you give him a chance to earn a dollar, he will think more of himself and more of you.

The only way to help people is to give them a chance to help themselves. So the Roycroft Idea is one of reciprocity—you help me and I'll help you. We will not be here forever, anyway; soon Death, the kind old nurse, will come and rock us all to sleep, so we had better help one another while we may. We are all going the same way—let's go hand in hand!

> **Don't take life too seriously—you'll never get out of it alive.**

His Final Days

A Story of
the Titanic

Elbert Hubbard wrote this story two years before his own death at sea on the Lusitania. The poignant eulogy he penned for Isador and Ida Straus applies equally to Elbert himself and his beloved wife, Alice:

"Mr. and Mrs. Straus, I envy you that legacy of love and loyalty left to your children and grandchildren. The calm courage that was yours all your long and useful career was your possession in death. You knew how to do three great things—you knew how to live, how to love, and how to die."

It is a night of a thousand stars. The date, Sunday April 14, 1912. The time, 11:20 p.m. The place, off Cape Race—that cemetery of the sea.

Suddenly a silence comes—the engines have stopped—the great iron heart of the ship has ceased to beat. Such a silence is always ominous to those who go down to the sea in ships.

"The engines have stopped!"

Eyes peer; ears listen; startled minds wait!

A half-minute goes by.

Then the great ship groans, as her keel grates and grinds. She reels, rocks, struggles as if to free herself from a titanic grasp, and as she rights herself, people standing lose their center of gravity.

"An iceberg!" someone cries. The word is passed along.

"Only an iceberg! Barely grated it—side-swiped it—that is all! Ah, ha!"

The few on deck and some of those in cabins peering out of portholes, see a great white mass go gliding by.

A shower of broken ice has covered the decks. Passengers pick up specimens, "for souvenirs to carry home," they laughingly say.

Five minutes pass. The engines start

again—but only for an instant. Again the steam is shut off. Then the siren-whistles cleave and saw the frosty air.

Silence and the sirens! Alarm, but no tumult. But why blow the whistles when there is no fog?

The cold is piercing. Some who have come up on deck return to their cabins for wraps and overcoats. The men laugh—and a few nervously smoke.

It is a cold, clear night of stars. There is no moon. The sea is smooth as a Summer pond. The great, towering iceberg that loomed above the topmost mast has done its work, gone on, disappeared into the darkness.

"There was no iceberg—you only imagined it," a man declares. "Go back to bed—there is no danger—this ship can not sink anyway!" says the Managing Director of the company.

In a lull of the screaming siren, a hoarse voice is heard calling through a megaphone from the bridge "Man the lifeboats! Women and children first!"

"It sounds just like a play," says Henry Harris to Major Butt.

Stewards and waiters are giving out life-preservers and showing passengers how to put them on.

There is laughter—a little hysteric. "I want my clothes made to order," a woman protests. "This is an outrageous fit!"

The order of the Captain on the bridge is repeated by other officers—"Man the lifeboats! Women and children first!"

"It's a boat-drill—that's all! A precautionary measure—we'll be going ahead soon," says George Widener to his wife, in reassuring tones as he holds her hand.

Women are loath to get into the boats. Officers, not over gently, seize them, and half-lift and push them in. Children crying, and some half-asleep, are passed over into the boats. Mother-arms reach out and take the little ones. Parentage and ownership are lost sight of.

Some boats are only half-filled, so slow are the women to believe that rescue is necessary. The boats are lowered, awkwardly, for there has never been a boat-drill, and assignments are being made haphazard.

A sudden little tilt of the deck hastens the proceeding. The bows of the ship are settling—there is a very perceptible list to starboard.

An Englishman, tired and blasé, comes out of the smoking-room, having just ceased a card-game. He very deliberately approaches an officer who is loading women and children into a lifeboat. The globe-trotting Briton is filling his pipe. "I say, officer;

> **God will not look you over for medals, diplomas, or degrees—but for scars.**

what seems to be the matter with this bloomin' craft, you know?"

"Fool," roars the officer, "the ship is sinking!"

"Well," says the Englishman, as he strikes a match on the rail, "Well, you know, if she is sinking, just let 'er down a little easy, you know."

John Jacob Astor half forces his wife into the boat. She submits, but much against her will. He climbs over and takes a seat beside her in the lifeboat. It is a ruse to get her in. He kisses her tenderly, stands up, steps lightly out and gives his place to a woman.

"Wait—here's a boy—his mother is in there!"

"Lower away!" calls the officer—"There is no more room."

Colonel Astor steps back. George Widener tosses him a woman's hat, picked up from the deck. Colonel Astor jams the hat on the boy's head, takes the lad in his arms, runs to the rails, and calls, "You won't leave this little girl, will you?"

"Drop her into the boat," shouts the officer. The child drops into friendly hands as the boat is lowered.

Astor turns to Widener and laughingly says, "Well, we put one over on 'em that time."

"I'll meet you in New York," calls Colonel Astor to his wife as the boat pulls off. He lights a cigarette and passes the silver case and a match-box along to the other men.

A man runs back to his cabin to get a box of money and jewels. The box is worth three hundred thousand dollars. The man changes his mind and gets three oranges, and gives one orange each to three children as they are lifted into safety.

As a lifeboat is being lowered, Mr. and Mrs. Isador Straus come running with arms full of blankets, brought from their stateroom. They throw the bedding to the people in the boat.

"Help that woman in!" shouts an officer. Two sailors seize Mrs. Straus. She struggles, frees herself, and proudly says, "Not I—I will not leave my husband." Mr. Straus insists, quietly and gently, that she shall go.

But Mrs. Straus is firm. "All these years we have traveled together, and shall we part now? No, our fate is one."

She smiles a quiet smile, and pushes aside the hand of Major Butt. "We will help you—Mr. Straus and I—come! It is the law of the sea—women and children first—come!" says Major Butt.

"No, Major, you do not understand. I remain with my husband—we are one, no matter what comes—you do not understand!"

"See," she cried, as if to change the subject, "there is a woman getting in the lifeboat with her baby; she has no wraps!" Mrs. Straus tears off her fur-lined robe and places it tenderly around the woman and the innocently sleeping babe.

William T. Stead, grim, hatless, with furrowed face, stands with an iron bar in hand as a lifeboat is lowered. "Those men in the steerage, I fear, will make a rush—they will swamp the boats."

Major Butt draws his revolver. He looks toward the crowded steerage. Then he puts his revolver back into his pocket, smiles. "No, they know we will save their women and children as quickly as we will our own."

Mr. Stead tosses the iron bar into the sea.

He goes to the people crowding the afterdeck. They speak a polyglot language. They cry, they pray, they supplicate, they kiss each other in frenzied grief.

John B. Thayer, George Widener, Henry Harris, Benjamin Guggenheim, Charles M. Hays, Mr. and Mrs. Straus, move among these people, talk to them and try to reassure them.

There are other women besides Mrs. Straus who will not leave their husbands. These women clasp each other's hands. They smile—they understand!

Mr. Guggenheim and his secretary are in full dress. "If we are going to call on Neptune, we will go dressed as gentlemen," they laughingly say.

The ship is slowly settling by the head. The forward deck is below the water. The decks are at a vicious angle. The icy waters are full of struggling people. Those still on the ship climb up from deck to deck.

The dark waters follow them, angry, jealous, savage, relentless. The decks are almost perpendicular. The people hang on by the rails.

A terrific explosion occurs—the ship's boilers have burst. The last lights go out. Darkness!

The great iron monster slips, slides, gently glides, surely, down, down, down into the sea.

Where once the great ship proudly floated, there is now a mass of wreckage in the great black all-enfolding night. Overhead, the thousand stars shine with a brightness unaccustomed.

The Strauses, Stead, Astor, Butt, Harris, Thayer, Widener, Guggenheim, Hays—I thought I knew you, just because I had seen you, realized somewhat of your able qualities, looked into your eyes and pressed your hands, but I did not guess your greatness.

You are now beyond the reach of praise. Flattery touches you not, words for you are vain. Medals for heroism—how cheap the gilt, how paltry the pewter!

Words unkind, ill-considered, were some times flung at you, Colonel Astor, in your lifetime. We admit your handicap of wealth—pity you for the accident of birth—but we congratulate you that as your mouth was stopped with the brine of the sea, so you stopped the mouths of the carpers and critics with the dust of the tomb.

If any think unkindly of you now, be

he priest or plebian, let it be with finger to his lips, and a look of shame in his own dark heart.

Charles M. Hays—you who made life safe for travelers on shore, yet you were caught in a sea-trap, which, had you been manager of that Transatlantic Line, would never have been set, baited as it was with human lives. You placed safety above speed. You fastened your faith to utilities, not futilities.

You and John B. Thayer would have had a searchlight and used it in the danger-zone, so as to have located an iceberg five miles away. You would have filled the space occupied by that silly plunge-bath (how ironic the thing) with a hundred collapsible boats, and nests of dories.

You, Hays and Thayer, believed in other people—you trusted them—this time they failed you. We pity them, not you.

And Mr. and Mrs. Straus, I envy you that legacy of love and loyalty left to your children and grandchildren. The calm courage that was yours all your long and useful career was your possession in death.

You knew how to do three great things—you knew how to live, how to love, and how to die.

Archie Butt, the gloss and glitter on your spangled uniform were pure gold.

> **That person has achieved success who has lived well, laughed often, and loved much.**

I always suspected it. You tucked the ladies in the lifeboats, as if they were going for an automobile ride. "Give my regards to the folks at home," you gaily called as you lifted your hat and stepped back on the doomed deck.

You died the gallant gentleman that you were. You helped preserve the old and honored English tradition, "women and children first." All America is proud of you.

Guggenheim, Widener and Harris, you were unfortunate in life in having more money than we had. That is why we wrote things about you, and printed them in black and red. If you were sports, you were game to the last, cheerful losers, and all such are winners.

As your souls play hide-and-seek with sirens and dance with the naiads, you have lost interest in us. But our hearts are with you still. You showed us how death and danger put all on a parity. The women in the steerage were your sisters—the men your brothers; and on the tablets of love and memory we have engraved your names.

William T. Stead, you were a writer, a thinker, a speaker, a doer of the word. You proved your case; sealed the brief with your heart's blood; and as your bearded face looked in admiration for the last time up at the twinkling, shining stars, God in pardonable pride said to Gabriel, "Here comes a man!"

And so all you I knew, and all that thousand and half a thousand more I did not know, passed out of this Earth-life into the Unknown, upon the tide. You were sacrificed to the greedy Goddess of Luxury and her consort, the Demon of Speed. Fate decreed that you should die for us.

Was it worth the while? Who shall say? The great lessons of life are learned only in blood and tears.

We should not feel sorrow for the dead. The dead are at rest, their work is ended, they have drunk of the waters of Lethe, and these are rocked in the cradle of the deep. We kiss our hands to them and cry, "Hail and Farewell—until we meet again!"

But for the living, who wait for footsteps that will never come again and who listen for a voice that will never more be heard, our hearts go out in tenderness, love, and sympathy.

These dead have not lived and died in vain. They have brought us all a little nearer together—we think better of our kind.

There are two good ways to die: one is of old age, and the other is by accident. But to pass out as did Mr. and Mrs. Isador Straus is glorious. Few have such a privilege. Happy lovers, both. In life they were never separated, and in death they are not divided.

Made in the USA
Las Vegas, NV
05 December 2024

13407465R00067